THE PANIC OF 1837

THE PANIC
OF 1837

*Some Financial Problems of
the Jacksonian Era*

REGINALD CHARLES McGRANE

Phoenix Books

THE UNIVERSITY OF CHICAGO PRESS
Chicago and London

THE UNIVERSITY OF CHICAGO PRESS, CHICAGO & LONDON
The University of Toronto Press, Toronto 5, Canada

PREFACE

In this study I have endeavored to describe the economic forces and the leaders involved in the great crisis of 1837. The close relationship between business and politics, the clashing ambitions of Andrew Jackson, Nicholas Biddle, and Martin Van Buren, and the dominant tone of Jacksonian democracy versus Whig aristocracy have been set forth. A perusal of these pages will, I hope, show the several stages in one particular business cycle and its concomitant political aspects.

I wish to express my deep gratitude to those who have assisted me in the preparation of the monograph. Professor F. L. Paxson of the University of Wisconsin suggested the possibilities of the field for research to me some years ago when I was a student in his seminar. The study was continued under the direction of Professors A. C. McLaughlin and W. E. Dodd, of the University of Chicago, who, by their helpful criticism, added to the many obligations I owe them. The grandsons of Nicholas Biddle, Edward and the late Charles Biddle, kindly placed at my disposal all the papers of their distinguished grandfather. My friend and colleague, Professor George A. Hedger of the University of Cincinnati,

v

has displayed his customary thoughtfulness and keen scholarly interest in offering many timely suggestions. I am also grateful to the staffs of the following libraries: Library of Congress, Pennsylvania Historical Society, Wisconsin Historical Society, New York Public Library, and Harvard University Library. The tedious task of preparing the manuscript for the publisher was performed by my wife, who helped me also in textual and interpretative criticism. However, I alone assume the responsibility for any errors which may have crept into the text.

R. C. McG.

TABLE OF CONTENTS

CHAPTER   PAGE

   I. An Economic Survey 1

  II. Land Speculation 43

 III. Biddle and the Recharter of the Bank . . 70

 IV. Financial and Industrial Aspects of the Panic 91

  V. Political Aftermath of the Panic . . . 145

 VI. The United States Bank and the Resumption of Specie Payment 177

VII. Struggle over the Independent Treasury Bill 209

Bibliography 237

Index 255

CHAPTER I

AN ECONOMIC SURVEY

The panic of 1837 was one of the most disastrous crises this nation has ever experienced. It was the culmination of a long train of events that extended back over a number of years. It marked the close of one epoch in our industrial history, and the beginning of a new era. It engulfed all classes and all phases of our economic life within its toils; and for seven long years the people of this land struggled to free themselves from its oppression. It revealed the weaknesses within our financial organization, while it brought upon the stage, for the last time, the three personages that dominated the political and economic arena of the thirties—Andrew Jackson, the westerner, Nicholas Biddle, the financier, and Martin Van Buren, the weak successor of an able protagonist. Andrew Jackson, with his political philosophy of the supremacy of the people, crushed the Bank of the United States in 1832, and thereby laid the foundation for the crisis of 1837; Nicholas Biddle, the brilliant representative of a distinguished family, recovered the sinking fortunes of his bank by obtaining a state charter, when a national charter was not available. Under his able guidance, the new institution and its followers rallied to the strife between bank and state. Martin Van Buren, by means of his sub-treasury scheme, added confusion to the already present chaos of these years. The contest between the cohorts of Andrew Jackson and Nicholas Biddle prepared the ground for the hard times of 1837; and the succeeding strife between the followers of Martin Van Buren and Nicholas Biddle prolonged the distress. Not until 1844 did the nation fully recover from the effects of this titanic struggle.

The year 1830 may be taken as a convenient starting-point for our story, for, with the close of the Napoleonic wars, with the great increase in the population of the country, with the rise of domestic manufactures, and with the gigantic schemes for internal improvements then prevalent, new demands were "created for labor, and new markets for farmers."[1] Jackson, in his messages of 1831 and 1832, triumphantly pointed to the "rare example of a great nation abounding in all the means of happiness and security."[2] Our finances were regulated by a bank that was respected both abroad and at home; our people were prosperous, contented, and boastful. Only the lowering cloud of nullification darkened an otherwise clear horizon when Jackson began

---

[1] Hildreth, *Banks, Banking, and Paper Currencies*, p. 82.

[2] *Cong. Debates*, Vol. VIII, Part III, App., p. 5; *ibid.*, Vol. IX, Part II, App., p. 4.

to question the constitutionality and advisability of a national bank. With the first omens of war, Biddle prepared for the duel that was to last throughout Jackson's two administrations. Resolving to protect his stockholders, the financier tried first to pacify his opponents; and when this failed, Biddle threw caution to the winds, and asked for the recharter of his bank four years before its expiration. Old Hickory accepted the challenge in his veto message of July 10, 1832; and straightway Jackson, the spokesman of prosperity, became the harbinger of distress.[1] The bank question became a political, rather than a financial, issue. The election of 1832 was a referendum on the subject. Left to the decision of an electorate in a heated campaign, the result was foreordained. It then remained to be seen how the "Monster of Chestnut Street" would respect the interests of the people, the administration, and the party at whose hands it had suffered.

The year 1833 commenced with brilliant prospects of continued national prosperity. Trade was profitable, the crops were good, and foreign and domestic commerce was thriving. Real estate in New York was rising, and money was abundant.[2] But beginning with the month in which the removal of deposits took place, Niles began to print doleful

[1] For this topic cf. McGrane, *Correspondence of Nicholas Biddle, passim.*

[2] Tuckerman, editor, *The Diary of Philip Hone*, I, 86.

sketches of the business world. "Money is scarce,"
Niles petulantly cried throughout October and November. "Stocks are falling," wrote Philip Hone,
under December 27. "A panic prevails which will
result in bankruptcies and ruin in many quarters
where a few weeks since the sun of prosperity shone
with unusual brightness." The whole community
began to groan under the financial hardships as the
friends of the United States Bank on one hand, and
the Jackson men on the other, struggled for control.
By December, laborers were being discharged, and
in January the news of the failure of business houses
and banks in Philadelphia, New York, and Washington were heralded in all the papers.

The Bank of the United States began to contract its loans on August 13, 1833, and abandoned
its policy of curtailment September 16, 1834.[1]
Against the solicitations of many of his most intimate friends,[2] Biddle determined to safeguard the
interests of his institution in the face of the government's "suicidal" actions. With mercantile houses
failing all about him, with the newspapers filled with
the shrieks of economic distress, and many of his
closest advisers upbraiding him, the financier continued his policy of curtailment in order, as he said,

[1] Catterall, *The Second Bank of the United States*, p. 314.

[2] McGrane, *op. cit.*, pp. 221, 241–43. On the other hand,
Biddle received requests from some of his friends to remain firm
in his opposition to the government (*op. cit.*, p. 227).

to safeguard the Bank and the nation at large. "If the bank remains strong and quiet, the course of events will save the bank, and save all the institutions of the country which are now in great peril," wrote Biddle to one of his friends. "But if, from too great sensitiveness, from the fear of offending, or the desire of conciliating, the bank permits itself to be frightened or coaxed into any relaxation of its present measures, the relief will itself be cited as evidence that the measures of the government are not injurious or oppressive, and the bank will inevitably be prostrated." His whole thought was how to salvage his own institution, confident that in so doing he would demonstrate to the people the blundering mistakes of the government. Already he was laying plans for obtaining a state charter for the old national bank, and when, at last, he deemed his own position secure, orders were given for the cessation of the war. Then the stringency in the money market was relieved, and by October, 1834, the worst was over.

By the spring of 1835 the country apparently had forgotten its past disorders. The price of cotton rose from 11 cents a pound in 1834 to 16 cents a pound in 1835.[1] The quantity of public lands sold in 1835 was three times the amount of 1834.[2] Not only

[1] Sumner, "A History of Banking in the United States," in a *History of Banking in All the Leading Nations*, I, 259.

[2] *Exec. Doc., Twenty-fifth Cong., Second Sess.*, Doc. 80. Land Office Report, January, 1838.

was the United States out of debt, but, largely through this amazing sale of the public domain, she was piling up a surplus in her treasury. The value of property in New York was higher than it had been for five years, business was brisk, and the city assumed a new aspect.

Under the guise of this new pretended wealth, the credit system was expanded among individuals and states. Men imagined they were in possession of wealth when, in reality, they possessed nothing but worthless promises. The first reversal in the commercial world was destined to be followed by a train of calamities. Biddle, the shrewd banker that he was, remembering the direful experiences of the panic of 1825, and the manner in which he had weathered the storm,[1] bided his time, while secretly strengthening his own house for any contingency. He fully realized that his opponent, Andrew Jackson, did not understand the intricacies of the financial market, and perhaps he suspected that his antagonist again would meddle with the situation. In this suspicion he was borne out. On July 11, 1836, came the ominous Specie Circular. Nervousness became apparent in the money market as the effects of the Specie Circular, in conjunction with the distribution of the surplus revenue, began to work. The next year saw the country in the throes of the great panic of 1837. The bubble of prosperity

[1] McGrane, *op. cit.*, p. 36.

made of fictitious wealth had at last been pricked. To appreciate fully the illusion of all sections and all classes in their fancied security, an extended account of the industrial, banking, and internal improvement schemes of these years is absolutely imperative.

The East, during the thirties, was the hub of the manufacturing industries of the country. Since the creation of the national government in 1789, this section had been the home of manufacturing, and by 1830 it was beginning to feel its strength. Iron and steel, cloth and leather manufactures, together with shipbuilding were fast forging to the front. By 1830, 202 furnaces were producing over 150,000 tons of iron valued at nearly $11,500,000; a decade later there were 804 furnaces producing 286,000 tons of cast iron, and valued at $22,750,000. One-half of these furnaces were located in New York and Pennsylvania.[1] So great was the interest in iron manufactures that the *American Railroad Journal* was established in 1831, devoted exclusively to railroad enterprises.[2] Factories were set up to supply the constantly growing demand for locomotives and railroad needs, and soon the Baldwin works at Philadelphia were doing a thriving business, with

[1] *Journal of the Proceedings of the Friends of Domestic Industry* (1831), p. 2; Bishop, *A History of American Manufactures, 1608–1860*, II, 423–24.

[2] Bishop, *op. cit.*, II, 363. By the East I mean the New England states, New York, Pennsylvania, New Jersey, and Delaware.

competitors appearing in other states. To encourage the mechanical arts, the New York Mechanics Institute was opened in 1833, where instruction was offered in modeling, machinery, architectural and ornamental drawing; and by 1835 New York alone could point to 112 cotton factories, 234 woolen factories, 13 glass, 63 rope, 70 paper, 24 oilcloth, and 293 iron works.

In New England one would naturally expect to find extensive manufacturing establishments, and this was certainly the situation during the thirties. Fall River, Massachusetts, where the first cotton mill had been erected in 1812, by 1833 contained thirteen cotton factories, one satinet factory employing 150 hands, besides numerous iron and nail shops. The yearly value of the manufactures of Middletown, Connecticut, was about $700,000, while the capital invested in similar enterprises in Lowell, Massachusetts, was over $6,000,000, where there were already twenty-two large cotton mills turning out annually 36,000,000 yards of cotton cloth.[1] One-third of the citizens were employed in the cotton factories, which was more than one-fourth of the whole number of persons employed in Manchester, the greatest cotton-manufacturing center in England, and probably the world. Women workers in the shops at Lowell received as high as $5 and

---

[1] Bishop, *op. cit.*, II, 377–79, 390; Pitkin, *A Statistical View of the Commerce of the United States of America*, pp. 523–24.

$6 a week, while few of their sisters in Europe could earn more than 20 cents a day, or $1 a week.[1] The shoe business and the woolen industry also were making great strides. The manufacture of leather was carried on to large extent in New York and Pennsylvania,[2] but Massachusetts likewise had a flourishing boot and shoe industry. By 1836, Lynn was manufacturing annually 2,500,000 pairs of boots and shoes, and its thriving condition was plain by the fact that between 1831 and 1840 forty-two streets were laid out within the town limits.[3] The woolen manufactures were also prosperous, while the hardware, bonnets and hats, soap, and candle men were well satisfied. In truth, a census of the manufacturing interests of Massachusetts on the eve of the panic disclosed that over $54,000,000 in capital had been invested in such undertakings; the whole number of hands employed was over 117,000, and the total value of manufactures was over $91,000,000.[4]

The industrial prosperity of the East necessarily advanced the demand for internal improvements. New York State, the progenitor of the Erie Canal, naturally took a prominent part in this mad desire

[1] Chevalier, *Society, Manners and Politics in the United States*, pp. 137–38.

[2] Pitkin, *op. cit.*, p. 496.

[3] Hazard, *The Organization of the Boot and Shoe Industry in Massachusetts before 1875*, pp. 63–64.

[4] Bishop, *op. cit.*, II, 409, 426.

for new means of communication. In the governor's
messages of 1832, 1835, and 1836 ample proof is
found of the pride of the people of New York in their
great canal system.[1] The canals gave employment
to a host of men and boys, and notwithstanding the
hard years of 1833 and 1834, the tolls increased
rather than decreased. The population of the larger
towns along the canals showed an advance of 50 per
cent in five years, which greatly strengthened the
demand for new projects.[2] The Erie Canal, connect-
ing the navigable waters of the lakes with the Hudson River, afforded an outlet for the produce and
trade of the interior counties. The Champlain Canal
connected Lake Champlain with the Erie Canal,
and furnished a means of egress to the products
accumulated around Lake Champlain, thus swelling
the tonnage and profits of the Erie Canal. The
Oswego, Cayuga and Seneca, Chenango, Crooked
Lake, and Chemung canals discharged upon the
main canal the vast resources centered in these interior lakes. The route of the Erie Canal, connect-
ing as it did the Great Lakes of the West and the
vast and fertile regions surrounding them with the
Hudson River and New York, possessed advantages
for the accumulation of revenue, as a thoroughfare
for trade and emigration, which was unequaled, per-

[1] Lincoln, *Messages of the Governors of New York*, III, 370,
462, 505.

[2] Pitkin, *op. cit.*, p. 547.

haps, in any part of the world.[1] Large sums of money were raised by lotteries in New York,[2] and a society was founded for the purpose of collecting and imparting information on all subjects connected with the advancement of the general system of internal improvements in the state.[3] The legislature became a willing tool in abetting the cause, and by 1840 Governor Seward could boast of 736 miles of canals and 406 miles of railroad completed under state supervision, exclusive of private turnpikes, macadamized and common roads. All the canals constructed by the state, except the Delaware and Hudson, were built by incorporated associations. The cost of these completed public works was over $12,000,000, which sum was borrowed chiefly at 5 per cent. The people were proud of their accomplishment, by which the navigable communication with the city of New York had been distributed over a territory of 25,000 square miles, a region equal to one-half the area of the state, and by 1840 sustaining more than one-half of its population. As the governor pointed out, their efforts in equalizing the local advantages of the different portions of the state was proved by the fact "that the average

[1] "Report of a Select Committee on the Public Debt of the State," *Journal of the House of Delegates of Virginia* (1839), Doc. 29, p. 4. The New York improvements were the subject of many discussions in other state legislatures, as this document is proof.

[2] *Journal of the Senate of Illinois* (1835), p. 240.

[3] *Boston Chronicle and Patriot*, January 23, 1836.

population per square mile of the regions not thus accommodated was only seven."[1]

The people of Massachusetts also demonstrated their interest in internal improvements. Massachusetts had constructed the first canal of any extent in the United States—namely, the Middlesex Canal, commenced in 1789 and completed in 1808—and had begun the first railroad, the Quincy, finished in 1827. The state, however, did not authorize loans for railroads until 1837, although several works had already been executed by private companies. In that year, state bonds were issued for the Western, Eastern, Norwich and Worcester, Andover and Haverhill, and Nashua and Lowell railroads in order to bring Massachusetts in touch with the commerce of the western states.[2]

In similar fashion, the state of Pennsylvania embarked upon gigantic undertakings. According to the *Pennsylvania State Register*, in 1831, over 700 miles of canals had been completed by the state and private companies; but by 1835 this number had swollen to 1,000 miles of canal, in addition to 640 miles of railroads, either finished or in the course of

---

[1] *Doc. Assembly of New York* (1840), I, 37, 38.

[2] Trotter, *Observations*, pp. 111–27. Little attention was paid to internal improvements by Maine, Vermont, New Hampshire, and Connecticut, and the few lines of railroads that were planned during these years were merely offshoots of the Massachusetts lines. Cf. Meyer, *History of Transportation in the United States before 1860*, pp. 143–45, 336–45.

construction. By the latter date, 265 miles of railroads had been constructed, which was more than
one-fourth of the whole extent of line then in use in
the United States. The Pennsylvania Canal and
Railroad extending from Philadelphia to Pittsburgh,
forming a connected line of communication 394
miles in length, was the most magnificent work of
the kind that had yet been completed in any part
of the United States.[1] The members of the state
legislature proved most pliable to outside pressure
when offered tempting internal improvements in
their districts, and Nicholas Biddle was to find this
an efficient means for securing desirable legislation.

In order to carry out these enterprises, which
were common to the eastern states, sufficient
funds were necessary. This needed money was supplied by the numerous banks which sprang into
existence between 1830 and 1836. Between 1830
and 1837, 347 new banks were chartered, 249 of
these new banks were located in the East, and
Massachusetts could lay claim to seventy-two of the
total figure.[2] During the same years, the banking
capital of Massachusetts rose from $20,000,000
to $40,000,000. Naturally, the money lent was also

[1] *American Almanac* (1832), p. 210; (1837), p. 227; Poor,
Sketch of the Rise and Progress of Internal Improvements, p. xxiii.
Chevalier, commenting on the Pennsylvania railroads, declares
the total length of all the railroads in France was only 94 miles.
Chevalier, *op. cit.*, pp. 85–86.

[2] *Hunt's Merchants' Magazine*, III, 458.

doubled. The debt due to the banks was correspondingly increased from $28,000,000 in 1830 to $56,000,000 in 1837. In the thirty years from 1803 to 1839, the population of Boston increased nearly threefold, while its banking capital increased eleven fold; the population of the country increased one and one-half fold, while its banking capital increased twenty-five and one-half times; and the population of the state increased one and one-half times, while the banking capital increased fifteen times. The circulation per head in Boston in 1839 was fourteen and one-half times greater than in 1803; five times that of 1803 in the country; in the whole state, four and one-half times that of 1803.[1] By January 1, 1837, the eastern banks had capital amounting to $62,000,000; loans, $98,000,000; specie, $2,000,000; and circulation $22,000,000.[2] But these figures tell only part of the tale. What was still more serious were the banking transactions of these institutions. In Maine, the bank commissioners discovered in some instances that loans had been made to stockholders before the capital had been paid in; in New York, that bank capital was paid in only to be borrowed by the stockholders under pledge of stock.[3] In Vermont one of

[1] *Hunt's Merchants' Magazine*, II, 159, 160.

[2] *Exec. Doc., Twenty-fifth Cong., Third Sess.*, Vol. I, Sec. of Treasury Report, 1838.

[3] Dewey, *State Banking before the Civil War*, pp. 14, 16.

the directors of the Bank of Bennington was connected with a firm of brokers in New York, and bought up notes of the bank at discount; while other banks in the state refused to allow the stockholders to examine their books, sometimes declared dividends when they had no profits to divide, and displayed doubtful favoritism in granting loans to customers.[1] In 1835 the circulation of the Connecticut banks bore the proportion to the specie of more than twelve and one-half to one; and an examination of certain banks revealed the fact that the banks had created fictitious deposits in order to increase their circulation; that certain bank presidents had drawn upon the funds of their banks both for purposes of the institutions and also for their own private use, and that when questioned regarding their transactions, frequently refused to produce the bank books for investigation.[2] In Massachusetts, the president and directors of the Commonwealth Bank were heavy debtors to their own institution, and recklessly indorsed the notes of their friends; while in other banks the habit had developed of buying their own stock at auction, and

---

[1] *Vermont Senate Journal* (1840), pp. xvii, xviii, xix. Report of Bank Inspector. On Vermont banks, cf. also *Senate Doc., Twenty-fifth Cong., Second Sess.*, Vol. VI, No. 471, p. 1006; *Journal of Senate of Vermont* (1837), App., p. 119; *Vermont House Journal* (1837), App., pp. 215, 216.

[2] *Exec. Doc., Twenty-fifth Cong., Second Sess.*, Vol. IV, Doc. 79, pp. 177–78, 190–98; Vol. VI, Doc. 471, p. 482.

selling it in advance with great laxness in the payment of such stock.[1] In Pennsylvania, several of the banks acknowledged, in 1837, that they were issuing ten paper dollars to every silver dollar they possessed; some of them fourteen to one; some twenty to one, and one of them thirty to one! Small wonder that with such transactions as these, the nation was soon flooded with worthless currency.[2] "To make a bank," Niles said, "is a great panacea for every ill that can befall the people of the United States, and yet it adds not a cent to the capital of the community."

The most perfect specimen we have of a deposit bank showing the demoralization and mischief produced by that system is the Girard Bank of Pennsylvania. It was founded in 1832; in 1834 it got a share of the public deposits. To make this share larger, an act of the Assembly was procured in 1836, increasing the capital from $1,500,000 to $5,000,000, and extending the charter twenty years. The stockholders gave the cashier two hundred shares of the stock for his agency in procuring the passage of the act. The increase in capital was paid by stockholders, and the bank was largely occupied in stock jobbing to carry out this operation. The maximum of government deposits having been obtained, a system of prodigality in loaning them out was commenced, which baffles the conception of sober and reflecting minds, and of which we have but few examples, even in the annals

[1] *Senate Doc., Twenty-fifth Cong., Second Sess.,* Vol. VI, Doc. 471, pp. 942, 945, 948–50.

[2] *Exec. Doc., Twenty-fifth Cong., Second Sess.,* Vol. II, Doc. 69, pp. 1–3; *Pennsylvania House Journal* (1837), Vol. II, No. 4, pp. 11, 12.

of modern banking. In fact, the paid-up capital was never over two-thirds of five millions but the government deposits ran at times as high as four millions. The assets consisted very largely of unavailable loans, so that with discounts of six to seven millions, scarcely two hundred thousand dollars was in active business capital.[1]

Conservative advice was unheeded by the public. Governor Marcy of New York, in his message of 1834, warned the state not to enlarge the banking superstructure without strengthening the foundation.[2] But his words were unheeded by the masses determined upon their own destruction. The market was soon flooded with paper money. Speculation of every sort in every kind of enterprise was rampant, from canals and railroads to real estate. The banks were willing to finance almost any conceivable proposal, and the people were willing to create more banks to satisfy their insatiate desire for money.

The hub of this activity in the East was New York City, and the importance of this city must not be underestimated. In 1835, New York was the first commercial city in the United States, and second in the world. Two-thirds of all the duties on imports were paid at its harbor[3] and one-fourth of all the exports passed through the same port.[4] Goods

---

[1] Sumner, *op. cit.*, I, 236, 237.   [2] Lincoln, *op. cit.*, III, 475.

[3] *Senate Doc., Twenty-sixth Cong., First Sess.*, Sec. of Treasury Report, 1839.

[4] Pitkin, *op. cit.*, pp. 451, 452.

loaded the wharves and blocked the streets, and crowds of merchants filled the hotels. Travelers marked the aspect of ease and cheerfulness of its citizens. The streets were wide and airy, the houses of the wealthier classes were decorated with taste, and the whole population bore the impress of opulence and prosperity.[1] Within six years, from 1830 to 1837, the value of real estate rose 150 per cent.[2] New York then, as it is now, was the great melting-pot of America. From fifteen thousand in 1829, the number of immigrants arriving at New York rose to sixty thousand in 1836.[3] Starting from this point they were distributed throughout the land, many of them going to the new states in the West. New York reflected the general tone and appearance of the East. It was wealthy, boastful, and improvident; and so was the whole section.

The second great area of the country was the South. The one great staple crop of the South was cotton, and upon this the wealth and good fortune of the region depended. New cotton lands were opened and cultivated in much the same manner as the East pushed forward its projects—namely, upon credit. The home consumption of cotton in 1831 was between 90,000,000 and 100,000,000

[1] Grund, *The Americans in Their Moral, Social, and Political Relations*, II, 77, 78.

[2] *Hunt's Merchants' Magazine*, VII, 452.

[3] Niles, July 8, 1837.

pounds, while by 1834 the exports amounted to 385,000,000 pounds, and were valued at nearly $50,000,000.[1] Investments in cotton brought good returns even in times of distress, and for many years it attracted a "large portion of the spare capital and labor of nearly half the territory of the Union." The great demand for cotton abroad made it our chief export, and in a degree the regulator of the balance of trade between the United States and Europe.[2] For the past five years (1830 to 1835) the crops had been promising, and everybody appeared prosperous.

The wealth of the South was even more illusory than that of the East. The South had to depend almost wholly upon a single crop, subject to the vagaries of nature, while all of the time the people were plunging deeper and deeper into debt. Slaves, tools, and machinery were bought upon credit.

Undeterred by these conditions, the planter, like his northern neighbor, entered courageously upon internal improvements. Governor Hayne, in his message of 1833, declared that South Carolina had expended nearly two million dollars in the construction of roads and canals which hardly yielded an

[1] Pitkin, *op. cit.*, p. 487; Sec. of Treasury Report, 1835, in *Senate Doc., Twenty-fourth Cong., First Sess.* By the South I mean all states south of the Mason and Dixon line, and east of the Mississippi River.

[2] Niles, January 7, 1832; *Senate Doc., Twenty-fourth Cong., Second Sess.*, Sec. of Treasury Report, 1836.

income sufficient to pay the current expenses; at the same time the Louisville and Charleston Railroad received hearty support from Calhoun and other leading men of the cotton belt.[1] In 1838 the governor of North Carolina declared the expenditure to carry out the system of internal improvements planned by the state involved a large sum, and that the people of North Carolina were too poor and too sparsely spread over the territory to command the means at once from their private resources to undertake such a task. Nevertheless, the governor boldly announced that the employment of the state's credit in foreign markets held "no higher terror to a mind of enlarged and patriotic views."[2] In the same year Georgia authorized a loan of $1,500,000 to complete the Western and Atlantic Railroad, which was to extend from Decatur across the Chattahoochee to the Tennessee River, where, in conjunction with other roads, the state would be brought into communication with the Tennessee River and Charleston.[3] Georgia's neighbor, Alabama, refused, however, to follow in the footsteps of her southern sisters. The people of Alabama were not lacking in enthusiasm for internal improvements but the state was unable financially to undertake such schemes. "State aid

[1] *American Almanac* (1835), p. 229; Trotter, *Observations*, pp. 223–27.

[2] *North Carolina Senate Doc.* (1838), No. I, p. 19.

[3] Trotter, *op. cit.*, p. 230; *Georgia House Journal* (1840), p. 112.

was thus regarded as unfeasible, in Alabama, during the very period when other states were most active in such work. Only small appropriations and loans were made to plank-road companies."[1] But Mississippi and Louisiana were not so hesitant; and by 1836 it was estimated that Louisiana would have 900 miles of railroads and 60 miles of canals under state supervision, outside of "private railroads and canals of considerable length on the estates of many planters."[2]

In 1832 the Virginia legislature had incorporated the James River and Kanawha Company and several railroad companies. The state took stock in most of these corporations, and appropriations were made to aid the Chesapeake and Ohio Canal, besides many other minor works. Within a few years large sums of money had been raised by the state. During this craze for internal improvements there were in the legislature two internal improvement parties, one much larger than the other, but both equally desirous of improving the state. The larger portion of the party was headed by "gentlemen of the first respectability and talents in the state, gentlemen who had devoted much of their time to the investigation of the subject of internal improvements."

[1] Martin, "Internal Improvements in Alabama," in *Johns Hopkins Studies*, XX, 31, 32, 40.

[2] *Mississippi House Journal* (1837), pp. 27, 28; *Mississippi Senate Journal* (1837), p. 44; *New Orleans Standard*, quoted in *Globe*, December 1, 1836.

They were willing to vote for any internal improvement scheme, and to borrow any amount to carry it out. The smaller portion of the party insisted that the money for these works be derived from taxation. Their arguments, naturally, were not welcomed, and the result was loan after loan made "without any means being provided to meet the interest annually, or to pay the principal when it should fall due." By these means a debt amounting in 1842 to about $6,500,00 was created, of which the citizens of the state held about $2,600,000, the banks of the state around $770,000, and the state and state institutions, over $1,000,000; in all, about $4,770,000 owed by the state of Virginia and her citizens.[1]

Maryland embarked more deeply in works of internal improvement "in proportion either to the extent of its territory, or to its population, than any other state in the Union."[2] In addition to the aid she gave the Chesapeake and Ohio Canal and the Baltimore and Ohio Railroad, Maryland entered upon an extended plan of internal improvement in 1836 by authorizing a loan of $8,000,000. Within the seven years succeeding the bank veto, the state

[1] *Virginia House Journal* (1842–43), Doc. 1, p. 2. This does not tell all the story. Besides the debts mentioned above, citizens of other states held Virginia bonds amounting to $610,000, and about $2,300,000 of the balance of the debt was held by subjects of Great Britain, France, Germany, and Switzerland.

[2] Trotter, *op. cit.*, p. 184.

debt was augmented more than $12,000,000. The governor later declared:

Within the same period, other roads and canals were projected, until . . . . we beheld the little state of Maryland having 10,000 square miles of territory, and 318,194 white inhabitants, staggering along with undertakings that would tax the financial resources of the whole kingdom of Great Britain. . . . . We were, at one and the same time, projecting or constructing a railroad to Annapolis, a railroad from Baltimore to Washington, a railroad from Baltimore to the Susquehanna, a railroad on the eastern shore, a railroad from Baltimore to the Ohio, and a magnificent canal from the tidewater on the Potomac to the Ohio River.[1]

Kentucky undertook the construction of turnpike roads and railroads, and improvements in the navigation of the principal rivers. The improvements on the rivers were undertaken exclusively by the state; but the railroads and the turnpike roads, with a few exceptions, were carried on in conjunction with incorporated companies. By 1839 Kentucky had expended over $3,000,000, could point to 464 miles of completed turnpike roads under contract, and in a state of progress, 343 miles more; making, in all, 813 miles of road; while portions of the Lexington and Ohio Railroad were open for service.[2]

Tennessee, not to be outstripped by her neighbors, authorized the governor in 1836 "to subscribe, on the part of the state, for one-third of the stock in

[1] *Maryland Senate Journal* (1839), pp. 45, 78; (1842), pp. 7, 8.
[2] *Kentucky Senate Journal* (1839), p. 25; *ibid.* (1840), pp. 33, 34; Trotter, *op. cit.*, p. 244.

any joint stock company that has been, or that may hereafter be, incorporated for the construction of railroads or macadamized turnpike roads within the limits of the state"; and by 1837 over a quarter of a million had been subscribed for such works.[1]

The spirit with which these enterprises were projected can well be portrayed in the utterances of the governor of Kentucky, even at a time when the fruits of these follies were becoming self-evident. "If all the turnpike roads under contract, and the whole improvements contemplated . . . . were completed," declared the governor, in 1839, "the whole debt of the state" would be a little over six millions. "What is this sum," exclaimed the exuberant executive, "to the resources and wealth of the state of Kentucky, whose taxable property is now valued at $275,000,000!"[2] Little wonder the South, in the years following the panic, was to feel heavily the tremendous drain upon her resources for these stupendous enterprises.

To finance these plans the South, like the East, resorted to extravagances in banking. Here, again, the southern planter outrivaled his northern brother in the scope and wildness of his schemes. From fifty-one banks in 1830, in the South, the number rose to eighty-two by 1837.[3] Few restrictions were

[1] *Tennessee Senate Journal* (1837), pp. 11, 12.

[2] *Kentucky State Journal* (1839), p. 25.

[3] *Hunt's Merchants' Magazine*, III, 458.

placed upon these institutions, with the result that they indulged in unbelievable practices. In 1830 the banking capital of Mississippi was $3,000,000; by 1839 it was over $63,000,000, yet the amount paid in was $26,000,000.[1] Mystery and concealment were the characteristic features of the banking processes of this state. Often the capital stock of the banks of Mississippi were paid in the notes of the stockholders. "Charters gave an opportunity for this in using the words 'secured to be paid.' The issues of the banks were consequently not issued upon what the stockholders had paid into the bank, but on what they owed to the bank, thus making their indebtedness, and not their actual capital, the basis of their circulation." In many instances the directors borrowed nearly the entire capital of their respective institutions, while all the banks gave heavy discounts to their officers.[2] By 1840 the bank commissioner could definitely state that he knew certain individuals were indebted to the banks of Mississippi for sums "of from one-half million to one million dollars, who, a few years previous, were not worth one dollar," but by virtue of the credit system they had been able to secure loans from the banks to purchase property. This property gave them additional credit, and "from one bank they proceeded to another, extending their credit and increasing

[1] *Mississippi Senate Journal* (1839), pp. 26, 27.

[2] *Ibid.* (1839), pp. 26, 27; (1840), p. 152.

their property at an enormous price," until they and the credit system broke down. From the bank commissioner's report of 1838 it was clear that a few persons had obtained control of the banks, and had made most of their loans to commission merchants, speculators, and officers of the banks; that the banks had applied most of their funds in the purchase of bills of exchange drawn on cotton monopolists, "and not predicated on funds in hand, or even expected at the time and place of maturity." The seventeen banks examined at that time had about $303,000 of specie in their vaults, and had made advances on cotton to the amount of $314,000, while their circulation amounted to more than $6,000,000, and their deposits to $1,000,000.[1]

Mississippi banks were not alone in these transactions. In Alabama "any one with a supply of cotton on hand might have it valued, and on delivering into the charge of the bank, receive an advance of not more than 25 per cent of the value, and then give his note for the amount received, payable in nine months." Similar practices were pursued by the Kentucky and Tennessee banks.[2] In Florida, loans were made to planters upon their slaves. There were no written mortgages, as the slaves

[1] *Senate Doc., Twenty-fifth Cong., Second Sess.,* Vol. VI, No. 471, p. 73.

[2] *Kentucky Senate Journal* (1837), pp. 212, 213; *Tennessee Senate Journal* (1841), p. 23; Dewey, *op. cit.,* pp. 21, 164, 165.

were simply enumerated as "Tom," "Dick," "Sally," or "Mary," with no further description, unless occasionally the age. Twenty years hence, neighbors might be found able to swear that certain negroes were the identical "Toms" and "Marys" that had been mortgaged to the bank on a given day, or that certain children were the progeny of these "Marys," but in case of doubt there was no documentary proof to solve the controversy.[1] In Georgia, bank charters were requested on the plausible ground that additional banking capital was demanded by the commercial necessities of the city or town in which it was proposed to establish the bank. The charter would be granted, and the incorporated gentlemen, to comply with the precautionary regulations of the legislature, borrowed, for a few days, the amount of specie required to be placed in the vaults before operations could be commenced. The bank would open under these auspices, the specie would be returned to its proper owner, and the notes of the stockholders would be substituted for it. On such unsafe, fraudulent, and unsubstantial foundations rested many of the Georgia corporations.[2] Furthermore, many railroad companies were chartered by the southern states with banking privileges, thereby increasing the already large number of such establishments.

[1] *Florida Legislative Council Journal* (1840), pp. 37, 38.
[2] *Georgia Senate Journal* (1841), p. 12.

The third great area in the Union was the West. This region, although much younger than either the East or the South, was becoming an important factor in the political and economic growth of the nation. The development of the West during the thirties was phenomenal. The states carved out of this territory possessed vast tracts of public land and unbounded resources which were draining the East of its settlers. The population of Ohio, Indiana, Illinois, Missouri, and Michigan was expanding by leaps and bounds. In 1826 the wealth of the manufacturing district of Cincinnati amounted, according to an accurate statistical examination, to $1,800,000, in a population of sixteen thousand. Nine years later its population had risen to thirty-one thousand; "more than 100 steam engines, about 240 cotton gins, upward of 20 sugar mills, and 22 steamboats" had been built during 1835.[1] Cincinnati was not only the "Porkopolis" of the West, but also the principal furniture center of this area. "In 1833 this industry ranked second only to machinery in that city. Large steam plants, employing a hundred or more hands had cheapened production until the Ohio metropolis commanded wide markets throughout the South and West."[2]

[1] Bishop, *op. cit.*, II, 394, 395; Hall, *Statistics of the West*, pp. 265, 269. By the West I mean Ohio, Indiana, Illinois, Missouri, and Michigan.

[2] Clark, *History of Manufactures in the United States, 1607–1860*, p. 474.

The first cylinder printing-press in the West was purchased the same year for the Methodist Book Concern of Cincinnati. Across the river, the Newport Manufacturing Company was employing two hundred hands, and manufacturing woolen goods, cotton bagging, cotton yarn, and bale rope to the value of $200,000. The manufactures of Covington were estimated at $500,000, where there was a large iron-rolling and nail works. Dayton, Ohio, in 1836, could boast of $1,000,000 invested in trade and manufactures. Here were located cotton mills, gun-barrel factories, the Dayton Carpet Factory, extensive machine shops, and iron, soap, candle, and clock establishments.[1] Pittsburgh, Louisville, Nashville, Chicago, Detroit, St. Louis, and numerous other towns strove with Cincinnati for the latter's title of the "Emporium of the West."[2] The migration to these cities was so large that the residents had difficulty in handling the prodigious influx of immigrants.[3] The price of land necessarily rose, during these prosperous years, beyond the fondest expectation of the wildest speculator. In 1836 Dayton built eighty-one new houses,[4] while there were numerous towns throughout the West

[1] Bishop, *op. cit.*, II, 394, 395, 404. The figures given above are round numbers.

[2] Hall, *op. cit.*, pp. 265, 269.

[3] *Chicago American*, June 20, 1835.

[4] Bishop, *op. cit.*, II, 404.

which two or three years previous contained one or
two log cabins—as, for example, Beardstown, Illinois—now numbered two or three hundred frame
and brick houses.[1] St. Louis listed 120 steamboats
with a tonnage of 15,000 in its trade. Carpenters,
bricklayers, plasterers, and mechanics of every description were confident of securing work in this new
Eldorado, and every steamboat brought crowds of
sober and industrious immigrants.[2]

To provide adequate means of transportation
for these newcomers, the West turned her attention
to internal improvements. The message of the
governor of Missouri typifies the westerner's attitude on this subject. "The sooner we begin," said
the governor in 1836, "the sooner shall we be in
the enjoyment of the advantages resulting from
them."[3] By the close of 1839, Illinois had expended
$11,600,000 in internal improvements; Indiana,
$11,890,000; Missouri, $2,500,000; and Michigan,
$5,340,000.[4]

The method employed by Illinois furthering
these plans is a good example of the procedure
adopted by most of the western states. The magnitude of the Illinois schemes exceeded the wants of
the people in as great a degree as its estimated cost

[1] *Maysville Eagle*, January 3, 1833.

[2] Niles, February 6, 1836.

[3] *Missouri House Journal* (1836), p. 34.

[4] Porter, *The West from the Census of 1880*, p. 555.

exceeded the resources of the state. With a trading capital of $2,500,000, Illinois entered upon one of the most gigantic designs of inland communication. As early as 1823 the state had conceived the project of connecting the Illinois River with Lake Michigan by means of a canal, "and a board of commissioners was appointed to explore the route and estimate the cost."[1] But no general system was outlined until 1837, when the legislature provided for a railroad from Galena to the mouth of the Ohio, from Alton to Shawneetown, from Alton to Mount Carmel, from Alton to the eastern boundary of the state in the direction of Terre Haute, from Quincy on the Mississippi through Springfield to the Wabash, from Bloomington to Pekin, and from Peoria to Warsaw, including in the whole about 1,300 miles of road. Appropriations were also made for the "improvement of the navigation of the Kaskaskia, Illinois, Great, and Little Wabash, and Rock rivers. And besides this, $200,000 were to be distributed among those counties through which no roads or improvements were to be made."[2] To realize the funds necessary for the prosecution of this immense system, the state issued bonds bearing 6 per cent interest, and reimbursable after a long term of years.

Such was the delusion of the times, that it was proposed to pay the interest as it would accrue upon these bonds by negotiating them in foreign markets and realizing the differ-

[1] Trotter, *op. cit.*, p. 315.   [2] Ford, *History of Illinois*, p. 184.

ence of exchange, by depositing the money thus raised with banks until it should be disbursed, and receiving premiums upon it; and by subscribing for bank stock, the dividends upon which it was expected would greatly exceed the interest upon the bonds with which the stock was purchased.

Thus it was contemplated . . . . to complete these extensive improvements without any expense to the state during their progress. When once in operation, it was maintained that they would yield a revenue not only sufficient for the payment of the interest upon the cost of their construction, but would furnish a surplus which might ultimately be applied to the liquidation of the principal.[1]

The citizens of Ohio also manifested much enthusiasm in internal improvements. In the session of the legislature of 1836–37, in order to encourage private enterprise, a law was passed "to the effect that when one-half of the stock of a turnpike, or two-thirds of that of a canal or railroad should be taken by individuals" the governor might, if the object was approved by the board of public works, subscribe the remainder in the name of the state.[2] Thus Ohio undertook to aid in the extension of the Miami Canal from Dayton to Defiance; for the Wabash and Erie Canal, from La Fayette on the Wabash to Manhattan near the mouth of the Maumee; for the Hocking Valley Canal, down the Hocking Valley to Athens; the improvement of

[1] Illinois, *Senate and House Reports* (1842), pp. 4, 5; cf. also C. Pease, *The Frontier State, 1818–48*, chap. xi, *passim*, on this subject.

[2] Trotter, *op. cit.*, p. 266.

the Muskingum River; the Walhonding Canal from Roscoe, in Coshocton County, up the Walhonding Valley; and the Western Reserve and Maumee Road. The estimated cost of all these works was $8,000,000 or one and six-tenths times the whole state debt at the end of 1837.[1]

The brilliant examples of Ohio and Illinois awakened a lively interest in the same subject among the citizens of Indiana. The first step was taken in 1835, when a survey of some ten routes was ordered. These surveys created much discussion of the whole topic of internal improvements, and at the next session of the legislature nine-tenths of the members took their seats virtually instructed to sustain the general proposition. Under these influences the internal improvement bill of 1836 was enacted, embracing a series of canals, macadamized roads, and railroads. The passage of this act was hailed by the newspapers as the beginning of a new era, celebrations were held in the villages, and an almost unbroken voice of approbation swept the state.[2] The cost of these works, which, as modified by a subsequent act, would comprise 840 miles of canal, 90 miles of railroad, and 335 miles of turnpike, was estimated at nearly $20,000,000.[3] To finance these

[1] Morris, "Internal Improvements in Ohio, 1825–50" in *American Historical Association Papers*, III, 128; Meyer, *op. cit.*, p. 289.

[2] *Indiana Senate Doc.* (1840), pp. 25–27.

[3] Trotter, *op. cit.*, p. 301.

works, two errors were committed. The first was the paying of most of the interest out of the money borrowed. This subjected the state to the payment of compound interest, and the citizens, not feeling the pressure of taxes to discharge the interest, naturally paid little attention to the policy pursued. "Had the legislature commenced by levying taxes to defray the interest as it accrued, its amount would have been a certain index to the sums expended on the works. This of itself would have done much to check extravagant expenditures." The second mistake was the selling of bonds on credit. Companies to whom bonds were sold on time were unable to fulfil their contracts when the money stringency swept the country. Too late, Indiana realized the follies of its former activities.[1]

Michigan, with a population but one-third of Massachusetts, was even more fanatical. Not admitted to the Union until 1836, in three years she had undertaken the construction of 1,000 miles of internal improvements at an expenditure of $8,000,-000. In addition to the public works constructed at state expense, twenty-four companies had been incorporated for building "as many different lines of railroads," whose united length was estimated to be over 1,000 miles, and to cost $6,000,000.[2] These

[1] *Indiana Senate Journal* (1841), pp. 13, 14, 17.

[2] Dearborn, *Letters on Internal Improvements and Commerce of the West*, p. 97.

were all designed to cross a peninsula bounded on
three sides by inland seas, affording the safest and
finest navigation in the land; and this was contemplated while four-fifths of the state was still a wilder-
ness! The system was altogether too extended for
the wants of its citizens, and required expenditures
beyond their means. Michigan was, unfortunately,
an easy victim to the spirit of the times, and with
a population less than 200,000, inhabiting a territory new and recently settled, with few immediate
resources but her credit, her enterprising head-
strong citizens planned a system of internal improvements which would have been a grand undertaking for the oldest and most wealthy state.[1]

Furthermore, the labor needed to carry on these
works in all sections of the country was drawn from
the productive industries of the nation. The temptation of high wages on the public works induced
the day laborers to abandon agriculture for more
profitable employment.[2] This meant a gradual
transfer of labor from the productive to the non-

[1] *Michigan Senate Journal* (1840), pp. 27, 28; (1841), Vol. I,
p. 167; (1842), Vol. II, pp. 25, 26.

[2] Niles, October 26, 1839. "These considerations prepare one
somewhat to find that the unemployed in 1837 seem to have been
for the most part unskilled laborers; that the demand for laborers
in the productive industries was not generally less than in 1835 and
1836; and that prices continued so high that the cost of the
workman's living averaged for the year only 8 per cent lower than
it was in October, 1836." Woolen, "Labor Troubles, 1834–37,"
in *Yale Review*, I, 99.

productive industries. This in turn caused smaller crops, higher prices, greater importation of wheat and rye, a larger surplus in the treasury, and more inflation and speculation. Certainly the West, with its ill-planned and poorly managed internal improved plans, contributed more than its share to the deceptive appearances of wealth.

To finance these plans, banks were created as by magic throughout the West. The banking practices of Michigan are an excellent example of the wildcat banks of this era in the West. On March 15, 1837, an act popularly entitled the "general-banking law of Michigan" was passed, upon the plausible principle of introducing free competition into what was considered a profitable branch of business heretofore monopolized by a few favored corporations.

In little more than one year, forty-nine banks were organized, with a nominal capital of $3,915,000, and about forty went into actual operation under its provision.

These institutions claimed to have an actual and available capital of $1,745,000; 30 per cent of the nominal capital was presumed to have been paid in, according to the law, in gold and silver; and they were authorized to put into circulation bank bills to the sum of $4,362,500, being two and a half times the amount of capital paid in and possessed. The feature of the act, authorizing banking under the suspension law (1837), that is to say, giving the sanction of law to the issuance of promises to pay

not liable to redemption in gold and silver on demand, gave an irresistible impulse to their career.

The loan of specie from established corporations became an ordinary traffic, and the same money set in motion a number of institutions. Specie certificates, verified
by oath, were everywhere exhibited, although these very
certificates had been canceled at the moment of their creation by a draft for a similar amount; and yet such sub-
terfuges were pertinaciously insisted upon as fair business
transactions, sanctioned by custom and precedent. Stock
notes were given for subscriptions to stock, and counted as
specie.

Thus, not a cent of real capital actually existed,
beyond the small sums paid in by upright and unsuspecting farmers and mechanics, whose little
savings and honest names were necessary to give
confidence and credit to these projects. The notes
of these institutions were spread abroad upon the
community in every manner and through every
possible channel; property, produce, stock farming
utensils, everything which the people were tempted
by advanced prices to dispose of, were purchased
and paid for in paper which was known to be
valueless.

Large amounts of notes were hypothecated for small
advances, or loans of specie, to save appearances. Quantities of paper were drawn out by exchange checks—that is
to say, checked out of the banks—by individuals who had
not a cent in bank, with no security beyond the verbal
understanding that notes of other banks should be returned
at some future time.

The result of this experiment of free banking in Michigan was to produce, at a low estimate, by 1839, nearly a million of dollars of the notes of insolvent banks due and unavailable in the hands of individuals.[1]

Laxness in banking practices was not confined to Michigan. In Ohio there were banks that gave no security for their circulation beyond their general assets, and when these banks failed, "the notes were in many cases found to be worthless." Then there were banks, such as the Bank of Gallipolis, that had been organized purely for speculation.[2] An investigation of the State Bank of Illinois after the crisis of 1837 disclosed the fact that Samuel Wiggins, a large stockholder, "had been allowed to use his bank stock as collateral for a loan with which to meet the payments due on it"; that the "cashier of the Chicago branch had loaned considerable sums to pork speculators, while accommodation was denied to others." Moreover, it was discovered that the "bank had lent its aid to ambitious schemes" for building up the commercial aspirations of Alton, Illinois, as a rival of St. Louis.[3] The State Bank of Arkansas was incorporated in 1836, and commenced

[1] *Michigan Senate Journal* (1839), pp. 191–93.

[2] Knox, *A History of Banking in the United States*, pp. 677, 678. These practices continued until 1843, and although the Bank of Gallipolis began in 1839, the same laxness was present as in the preceding period.

[3] Pease, *The Frontier State, 1818–48*, pp. 309, 310.

banking operations in 1837. Owing to the suspension of specie payments, it was forced to curtail its business, and not until December, 1838, did it actually begin.

At that time it was without a cash capital in its vaults, its only means consisting of certificates of deposits in other banks to the amount of $355,756.15, and $53,747.75 in the bills of other banks. Yet its charter provided for an original cash capital of $2,000,000. Moreover, the officers and stockholders of the bank, in utter disregard of the avowed object for which the bank was established, "to aid the great agricultural interests of the state, and the wants and necessities of the people," without having deposited any portion of their capital in the bank, sold and exchanged a very large proportion of the capital and funds of the bank and appropriated to themselves large sums of money; thus they allowed their debts to lie unpaid, and the paper to depreciate in value until it hung like an incubus upon the state, paralyzing its energies and retarding its growth.[1]

In sharp contrast to these institutions, the State Bank of Indiana stood forth as a shining example of conservative banking. "No bank in the country stood higher than did the State Bank of Indiana during the panic. In all the western and southern states its notes commanded a premium, and in the East were taken at a small discount." This was largely owing to the fact that its loans were made in small amounts, and scattered over the entire state.[2]

[1] *Arkansas House Journal* (1843), pp. 61–63; App., pp. 2, 3.

[2] Knox, *op. cit.*, p. 696.

There was a close connection between the expansion of bank circulation and our imports and exports. Between 1832 and 1834 the currency increased from $59,000,000 to $94,000,000, and the imports increased in value from $101,000,000 to $126,500,000; from 1834 to 1836 the currency expanded from $94,000,000 to $140,000,000 and the imports rose from $126,000,000 to $189,000,000. In the latter year (1836) the excess of imports over exports was upward of $61,000,000, and in 1837, $23,500,000. The import of the single article of silk in 1837, a mere luxury, amounted to $23,000,000, while our export of flour during the same year was about $7,000,000.[1] In the face of this unfavorable balance of trade, large debts were incurred abroad, due to the speculative fever then prevalent in England. The high rates of interest paid for the use of capital in America induced English capitalists to aid Americans in financing their operations in this country. Three English houses had extended credits to America to the enormous amount of nearly $19,000,000. These credits[2] were unquestionably increased during 1836

[1] *Sen. Doc., Twenty-fifth Cong., Second Sess.*, Vol. I, Doc. 2, *passim*, Sec. of Treasury Report, 1837; *Report to Senate and House of Illinois* (1842), II, 186, 187; *Pennsylvania Senate Journal* (1841), p. 22; Exports and Imports in *Sen. Doc., Twenty-sixth Cong., First Sess.*, Doc. 2 (Sec. of Treasury Report, 1839).

[2] Bank Commissioners Report, 1838, *N.Y. Assembly, Sixty-first Sess.*, Doc. 71, pp. 3–5.

by the extraordinary importations of breadstuffs. In the autumn of 1836, however, banking discredit commenced in Ireland, quickly followed by difficulties of the Northern and Central Bank of England; in January, 1837, a London banking house became embarrassed. The Bank of England was called upon to aid these institutions, and just as this discredit was hanging over the banking interests in London, the Bank of England began to grow suspicious of the financial transactions of the American houses in London and Liverpool.[1] As the Bank of England began to press the latter to meet their obligations, a sudden check was given to American credit in Europe. This threw back upon the United States a large amount of protested bills, thereby creating a threatening demand for specie to export, which immediately raised it to a premium, while the same causes operated to depress the great staple of the country in the market abroad, thereby rendering "in a great measure unavailable the only means of remittance actually possessed, except the stock of specie." The immediate cause of the run upon the banks which resulted in the suspension of specie payments was this foreign demand for specie.[2] The foreign demands coinciding as they did with the momentary transactions

[1] *Report of Select Committee on Banks of Issue*, House of Commons (1840), pp. 113, 114.

[2] *New York Assembly, Sixty-first Sess.*, Doc. 71, pp. 3–5.

had been unsettled by the workings of the Specie Circular, confidence was destroyed, and the crash became imminent.

Thus the East, West, and South joined hands in setting the stage for the panic of 1837. The questionable banking practices and extravagant internal improvement schemes of the East were duplicated by similar fantastic operations in the West and South. The universal prosperity of the nation led individuals and states to expand too rapidly the credit system, now that the restraining influence of the United States bank had been removed. The deceiving appearances of wealth during these flush days of the thirties led to excesses in banking and internal improvement projects; and another fruitful field for speculative purposes, as the next chapter will portray, was the public-land sales of these years.

CHAPTER II

LAND SPECULATION

One of the most prevalent forms of the speculative mania that infected the Americans of the thirties was connected with the occupation and sale of the public lands. The various phases of this malady, the efforts of the administration to curb and check it, the relation of the governmental officials with the speculator, and the final actions of the administration which stopped these operations are of especial interest in view of the light they throw on the speculation throughout the nation on the eve of the panic of 1837.

All classes and all sections of the country were guilty of the same offense, all were impelled by the same craze for speculation. The farmer, the manufacturer, and the merchant, instead of paying their debts, bought land and speculated in land. The conservative eastern capitalist, the reckless easygoing southern planter, and the wary, doubtful western farmer joined hands in their efforts to purchase land. Villages and cities sprang up over night in every direction, lots increased at the rate of 200 and 300 per cent per year, fortunes were made and lost in a few moments. All who had money or credit plunged headlong into the stream. Companies were formed, and through the generosity of the banks the mad rush to destruction was facilitated. The face of the country was checkered with new, well-mapped boom cities. The sale of the public lands for 1834 was 4,658,000 acres; for 1835, 12,564,-000 acres; and for 1836, 20,074,000 acres.[1] Naturally the increase in sales enlarged the amount of public deposit, and this in turn stimulated the banks to extend still further their issues. The public deposits, by the close of 1836, amounted to $49,000,000, while the deposit banks, with an aggregate capital of $77,000,000, showed discounts to the sum of $115,-000.[2] But in this transaction, as Jackson pointed out, the government received little more than credit on the books of the bank. "The receipts from the public lands were," as the President stated, "nothing more than credits on the bank. The banks let out their notes to speculators, they were paid to the receivers, and immediately returned to the banks to be sent out again and again, being merely instruments to transfer to the speculator the most valuable public lands. Indeed, each speculation furnished means for another."[3]

Public men, representing both parties, reiterated and strengthened Jackson's contentions. Represen-

[1] *Exec. Doc., Twenty-fifth Cong., Second Sess.*, Doc. 80.

[2] Sec. of Treas. Rept., 1836, *Exec. Doc., Twenty-fourth Cong., Second Sess.*, Vol. I, Doc. 4.

[3] *Cong. Deb.*, XIII, Part II, App., p. 6.

tatives and senators from the West called attention
to the hardship the connection between the banks
and the speculators necessarily had upon the settlers. The land office report substantiated these
charges of connivance between certain of the land
offices and the land grabbers.[1] Unquestionably,
speculation and bank juggling often went hand in
hand.

The craze was not confined solely to the West
and the public-land sales. The rise in the value of
real estate in New York was one form the speculative
spirit assumed in the East. From $250,000,000 in
1830, the valuation of real property in New York
rose to $403,000,000 in 1835, being an increase of 50
per cent in five years.[2] "The eagerness for land,"
declared Miss Martineau, "is extraordinary."[3]
"The rage for speculating in lands in Long Island,"
wrote Hone in his diary for January 24, 1835, "is
one of the bubbles of the day. Men in moderate
circumstances have become immensely rich, merely
by the good fortune of owning farms of a few acres
of this chosen land." Roswell L. Colt, the intimate
friend and close financial adviser of Biddle, likewise
commented on the same phenomena. "The money
market is in a feverish state," the latter wrote on
July 20, 1836, yet "real estate in the lower part of

[1] *Exec. Doc., Twenty-sixth Cong., First Sess.*, Vol. II, Doc. 12.

[2] *Report on Finances and Internal Improvements of the State of
New York* (1838), App., p. 6.

[3] Martineau, *Society in America*, II, 271.

the city maintains its price" and "lots 25 by 100 [feet] are worth and will bring ten to twelve thousand dollars a lot." Governor Marcy also called attention to the facts, and dealt at length with the speculative fever in his message of 1836. "Our citizens," proclaimed the chief executive, "who have been influenced by this spirit, have not confined their operations to objects within our own state. They have made large investments in other states of the Union." Yet large as these transactions were, they bore no comparison to the speculation "in stocks and in real property within our own state."

The vacant lands in and about several of our cities and villages have risen, in many instances, several hundred per cent. . . . . More by the competition and speculation than any real demand resulting from the increase in our population and actual prosperity. That the sudden rise in the price of these lands is ascribed to the true cause is evident from the conceded fact, that most of them have been purchased, not for the purpose of being occupied by the buyers, but to be again put in the market, and sold at still higher prices.

Moreover, the passion prevailed, as the governor pointed out "not only among capitalists, but among merchants and traders." The funds of these capitalists were withdrawn "to some extent from situations in which they afforded accommodations to business men," thereby obliging men to press upon the banks to supply this deficiency in their wants. In like manner, merchants and others "abstracted from their business a portion of their capital and devoted it to speculation in stocks and lands," and then "resorted to the banks for increased accommodation."[1]

The timber lands of Maine became a favorite habitat for the speculator of the East. The rumor "that the timber of Maine was diminishing so rapidly that the supply must soon be exhausted" precipitated the scramble to engross what remained. "The rage to purchase these lands became excessive, and most extravagant prices were paid."[2] Building lots in Bangor, Maine, which heretofore had sold for $300, now brought $800 and $1,000, while woodlands, instead of selling at their normal price of $5 and $10 per acre, were snatched up at the fanciful figures of $15 to $50 per acre.[3] The problem became so serious in Maine that the legislature took up the question of regulating these transactions. Grants of land for townships carried with them regulations providing for their survey within three years, their division into two hundred acre lots (or less), the erection and operation of a good sawmill and gristmill; the settlement of at least ten families upon separate lots, and within seven years, thirty families, and within ten years, fifty families; the erection of three comfortable

[1] Lincoln, *op. cit.*, III, pp. 555–57.

[2] Hildreth, *op. cit.*, p. 91.   [3] *Maysville Eagle*, July 16, 1833.

houses, and the payment into the treasury of the state of $3,500 in four equal payments with interest annually.[1] Even with these rigid requirements the legislature realized that many of the grantees failed to secure the necessary settlers, and used the operation solely as a speculative venture.

In similar fashion, other eastern districts were visited by the fever. Erie, Pennsylvania, Boston, Baltimore, and Buffalo, and numerous other cities were smitten by the malady, with the result that real estate soared to unheard-of heights, and lots brought fabulous sums.[2] In truth, the whole East lay under the spell of the speculator's magic wand, and land rose and fell according to his wishes.

In the South, as in the North, speculation was not limited to one separate area. Vicksburg imitated New York in its real estate transactions. One observer remarked that "dwelling-houses of the most indifferent character let for what they could be built at Cincinnati, and sell for what used to be thought an extravagant price for a splendid edifice on Broadway."[3] But the main speculation of the South centered in its sale of public lands, and, in this connection, the eastern capitalist showed his superior wisdom and organization in invading the southern domain. Such states as Mississippi, Lou-

[1] Sprague to Strong, November 8, 1831, Strong MSS.
[2] Niles, May 9, June 6, 13, 1835; October 22, 1836.
[3] Cox to Kemper, January 13, 1837. Bishop Kemper MSS.

isiana, Alabama, Arkansas, Georgia, and Kentucky clearly demonstrate the workings of their schemes.

In 1835 the New York and Mississippi Land Company was formed by a group of eastern capitalists to buy up the lands of Mississippi, and the accounts sent to the East by the young agent in control are very illuminating on the condition of sales in this state. Writing on December 12, 1835, he speaks of the great effort made at the public sale to stop competition among those present "so that the lands might be bought at low prices, but only with partial success." The capitalists, by bidding against each other, forced the sales up, with the result that "inferior lands brought high prices." The following month, the agent stated that there was one million dollars for investment at Pontotoc, Mississippi, and that this had caused the price per acre to rise from $1.25 to $2.50 per acre. Both western and southern capital were represented at this sale, which shows that the greed for land was not confined solely to the New York and Mississippi Land Company or its brethren of the East.[1] Eastern financiers were well informed of the proceedings of the sales in this vicinity, for Biddle received numerous requests to embark on these undertakings from buyers on the ground.[2]

[1] Bolton to Curtis, December 12, 1835; January 8, 1836, N.Y. and Mississippi Land Company MSS.

[2] Hubbard to Biddle, September 30, 1836; April 21, 1837, B.P.

The best evidence on the method pursued by the speculator in Mississippi can be found, however, in the senate report of March 3, 1835. According to the testimony given in the course of the investigation of the Chochuma sales, the procedure was somewhat as follows:

On the morning of the second and third days of the sales, a short time before the sales were open, R. J. Walker called the attention of the people before the tavern door about thirty yards from the land office, and read an arrangement, announcing that a company was formed to buy the land, and that such settlers as would comply with the terms proposed by the company should be protected; the settlers were to abstain from bidding; were to give into the company of speculators the number of the land, and one-eighth of the land, including the settlers' improvement, was to be transferred to the settler on his paying on the day it might be sold, the amount to be paid to the United States; and if one-eighth of a section would not cover the improvement, then the settler was to have one-fourth section.

In general, the people deemed it best "to close with the terms offered to them." A few persons refused, and some of these were forced to pay as high as $10 per acre.[1] After the company had finished its purchases, the settlers were disposed of:

The settlers' lands were portioned off to them, agreeably to the first and main designs of the company, and the residue

[1] American State Papers, *Land*, II, 495, 496. A good illustration of the manner of conducting these sales is found in the following extract from the same volume. "One of the public criers on the part of the United States . . . . and I understand to

was then put up at public sale, and was sold to the highest bidder, without any fixed price other than the first cost of the same. . . . . For the lands sold the company received various prices, from one dollar and a quarter up to six and seven dollars per acre, and in one instance of a supposed town site, $20 per acre.

At this particular sale, it was estimated that the financial loss to the government by the actions of the speculators was between $65,000 and $70,000.[1]

Another interesting fact which was clearly demonstrated by the senate report was the part played by certain land officials in some of these sales. The best example of this is found in connection with the Mount Solus sales in Mississippi.

The register and receiver at this land office, Samuel Gwin and George P. Dameron, were notoriously engaged in extensive speculations in land of the United States. In order to secure the most valuable tracts of land, of which they became possessed of accurate information by their official stations, they marked every such tract with the letter *S*, so that if the person wishing to purchase should apply for either of the tracts thus marked, the applicant was informed that the tract was previously entered, and in this manner it remained unsold until they, or either of them, could make a suitable profit by private sale, or found it convenient to pay the minimum price and obtain a final certificate of purchase.

---

be one of the speculators, and who resides in Alabama, when opposition bids were made, would frequently stop crying the land, and say, 'Gentlemen, you had better compromise among yourselves; you are fooling away your money.'"

[1] *Op. cit.*, pp. 479, 490.

Moreover,

These officers were in the constant habit of selling the public lands to applicants on credit, exacting from the purchaser a separate note as a "bonus" or interest on the nominal amount of the purchase money, which they appropriated to their own use, and signed a receipt for the purchase only when the money and interest were paid, and in the meantime the tract thus fraudulently sold was marked with letter *S* to prevent persons from making applications to enter it.[1]

Eastern capital and the southerner's laxity and natural willingness to take a chance transformed the Southland into a Garden of Eden for the land grabbers. Congressmen in Washington might thunder about flush times in the South, and the danger thereof, but so long as nothing disastrous happened, the South was content to revel in its pretended wealth.

Meanwhile the speculative mania invaded another territory. The underlying cause for the tide of migration westward, and its consequent effect upon the internal projects of the western states was the disposal of the public lands within their domains. Each land sale within its area brought a crowd of strangers and capitalists ready to avail themselves of the rapid rise in value of the real estate within this region. There was the poor immigrant desirous of securing a home, while along with him came the eastern capitalist intent upon monopolizing the soil

[1] *Op. cit.*, pp. 733–34.

for his own specific advantage. The idea prevailed
in the East that the western settlers, having already
pre-empted land without legal authority, were a
body of pirates, robbers, and outlaws, totally un-
worthy of the protection of Congress. The speculator possessed no feeling in common with the settler;
he beheld the settler, and the settler in turn beheld
him, with an envious, jealous eye. He did not meet
with a very cordial reception as he traveled among
them; and quite frequently he found his efforts
frustrated by their exertions.[1] But with his command of ready money he quickly secured the choi-
cest locations notwithstanding these obstacles, and
thus he and his cohorts swooped down upon this
area like a swarm of locusts.

One of the best states to study for the working of
this mania is Illinois. The large amount of refuse
land in the state afforded abundant occasion for
investments, while the ever increasing stream of
migration westward stimulated the desire to possess
land. By 1835 Illinois was in a most prosperous and
flourishing condition.

In 1836 lots in Quincy sold as high as $78 a front foot.
In April, 1837, desirable town lots in Monmouth were worth
$1,000. Less desirable ones were selling at the rate of $75 to
$100. In Peoria, at the same time, the best lots sold for $100
a front foot; and in March, 1837, there were twelve or fourteen houses within sight of Kickapoo Prairie, where nine

[1] Skinner to Van Buren, January 3, 1837, Van Buren MSS.

months before there was not a house. . . . . On the way to Savanna, in Carroll County, Dayton, Cleveland, Portland, Lyndon, and Union Grove had all been laid out in 1836, most of them having from three to twelve houses, with lots selling at from $10 to $125. On the road to Galena, Grand Detour and Dixon had been laid out in 1836. In 1839 they were towns of fifty houses, and the most desirable lots in them and in Oregon were held at from $400 to $600.[1]

Population and wealth were pouring into the state from the East, and great quantities of land were entered "both by residents and non-residents."[2] Land about Chicago brought large sums.

Naturally, numerous examples of frauds were perpetrated by speculators upon unsuspecting purchasers. It was claimed the land about Chicago was "sold and resold and sold again" in New York. Paper towns were laid out and advertised in the East as being at the "head of navigation" or the "handsomest location for a city in the world." The lots of many of these towns "today are the sites of some farmer's field."[1] Kankakee City, Illinois, was an outgrowth of speculation, and is a good illustration of this mushroom type of town. "In its best days the population numbered seventy-five; lots were sold in New York and Chicago for thousands of dollars, but the city fell with a crash in 1837, and today the site of the once promising Kankakee City is a farm." Grundy, Iroquois, DeKalb, Carroll,

[1] Pease, *The Frontier State*, pp. 176, 177, 190.
[2] *Illinois Senate Journal* (1838), p. 52.

Bureau, and Wills counties furnish additional instances of these paper towns.[1] Between Grand Haven and Grand Rapids, in Michigan, Port Sheldon was planned along the same lines.

It was started by capitalists of New York and Philadelphia, and a city of 124 blocks was laid out. An elegantly engraved map was made of the city and harbor, and widely circulated. Roads were cut; a charter was obtained for a railroad, a lighthouse was built, and a hotel was erected at a cost, it is said, of from thirty to forty thousand dollars; fifteen thousand dollars were expended on a mill; fifteen small dwellings were built.

It fell with the crash of 1837, and "it is said the hotel and thirty lots were sold for less than the cost of the glass and paint, and that the remainder of the land was bought for its hemlock bark."[2]

The city of High Bluffs, on the east bank of the Kaskaskia, promoted by a Canadian Frenchman, was another of these undertakings. The plan of the city was drawn by a skilled draftsman at St. Louis, and represented the city as situated in the most beautiful natural surroundings, on high ground gradually declining in grade to the river. The lots were numbered far into the hundreds, with finely embellished parts, and here and there a graceful church edifice. On two corner lots were pictured solid-looking bank buildings of Gothic architecture, and on others were schoolhouses, colleges, hotels, and hospitals. Near the river were shown great warehouses, two mills, and various factories. A heavily laden steamboat was depicted approaching the wharf from below; other boats were at the landing. . . . . All of that

[1] Pooley, *Settlement of Illinois*, pp. 385, 458, 564, 565.
[2] Fuller, *Economic and Social Beginnings of Michigan*, p. 439.

was lithographed on large sheets of heavy paper in the highest style of art. Supplied with a number of copies, the promoter left for the eastern cities in the fall. He returned in early spring by way of New Orleans and the Mississippi, with an immense stock of miscellaneous merchandise he had received in exchange for his city lots, which he converted into cash as speedily as possible. He was not at home when agents of eastern mercantile houses came West to look up their city property.[1]

Travelers of the period frequently warned the people against such maneuvers, declaring that many a buyer would esteem himself fortunate if, upon examination of his purchase, he found it not only unfit for cultivation but even unsuited for habitation. The justice of this accusation is proved in the case of Marion City, Missouri. This was another of the well-mapped cities of the era. Many of the lots in the city were sold in the East at from $200 to $1,000. When some of the investors sought the location, they found Marion City was just six feet out of water.[2]

Necessarily, grievous accusations were placed at the door of the speculator for such unbecoming actions. One general complaint was the method which they employed in securing their land. Not

[1] Snyder, *Life of A. W. Snyder*, pp. 181, 182. Other citations of a similar character can be found in *Voters and Taxpayers of DeKalb County, Illinois*, pp. 102, 103; *History of Carroll County, Illinois*, p. 123; Gross, *Past and Present of DeKalb County*, I, 46.

[2] Chevalier, *Society, Manners, and Politics*, p. 307; *Bishop Kemper's Diary*, March 25, April 27, 1836.

only did the eastern speculator have the opportunity of outbidding the poor settler, but he often had the advantage of a superior knowledge of the land he was buying. How true this was, in certain cases, can be determined from the correspondence of Moses M. Strong, for many years a land agent for certain eastern capitalists in Wisconsin territory. Writing to his promoters on one occasion, he related the experience of a young man who secured the position of surveyor and traveled through the West "taking notes of the country" as he carried on his work. Thus, wrote Strong, "when the land comes into market he can, of course, buy to better advantage than any other person." So forcibly did this impress the men of the East that pressure was at once brought to bear to secure a similar position for Strong, and after convincing Robert T. Lytle, the surveyor-general of Ohio at Cincinnati "that Mr. Strong was a friend of the present administration," the appointment was made, and Strong proceeded to carry out his well-laid plans.[1]

Another practice which called forth public condemnation was the alleged connivance between state legislatures and big land purchasers. This was a favorite cry among the opponents of the existing congressional land policy. Some justification for this assumption is shown in the writings of certain

[1] Strong MSS., November 16, 1835, January 21, 23, April 20, 27, 1836.

contemporary observers. One such commentator, whose veracity is unquestionable, speaks of promoters spending some time in Indianapolis in order to further their interests. How far the promoting of their own interests "involved doubtful transactions," or how far the practice was general, it is impossible to assert with any degree of assurance; but that the speculators exerted influence on the legislatures of certain states was probably true. It is quite certain that various state officials, such as Governor Duncan of Illinois, were not adverse to speculation, which goes to prove how deeply the disease had penetrated the body politic.[1]

Why did not the treasury department and the registers at the land offices restrain and control these practices? In endeavoring to answer this question we gain a clearer insight into the weaknesses of the governmental policy, and thereby into the devious methods employed by the speculators in their iniquitous work. The treasury department, from the beginning of the increased sales in the thirties, was most explicit in its instructions to the registers regarding the disposal of the public domain. The registers were informed regarding the kinds and specifications of township plots they were to use, their commissions, powers, and duties; whom the department considered "actual settlers"; and the department's and administration's solicitude

[1] *Bishop Kemper's Diary*, January 25, 1837.

respecting the proper use of the public land.[1] But notwithstanding this close and rather careful supervision by the main office, the men in charge in Washington were well aware of the many abuses practiced by the registers. The country people, when speaking of the land offices, frequently declared they were the "dens of thieves and robbers, a curse to the nation, and the destroyer of morals."[2] And a careful study of the land offices verifies this charge.

The best evidence on the method pursued by the speculator can be found in the report made to the Senate on March 3, 1835, respecting the Zanesville, Ohio, land office. The land office report for 1833 had called attention to the condition of affairs in this locality. A committee was appointed to investigate these charges, and a year later they made their report, including the following statement:

The committee have received but little evidence of frauds committed or tolerated by the land offices northwest of the Ohio River. These may nevertheless exist; but as no strong representations had been made on the subject, commissions for taking testimony had been sent only in the district of Zanesville, in Ohio. The evidence from that quarter shows a few cases of favoritism in the entry of public lands at private sales; and, at the same time, the practice generally prevailed of making the land offices depositories of

[1] *Registers and Receivers, New Series*, VI, 19, 78, in chief clerk's office, Land Office, Washington, D.C.

[2] Hubbard to Van Buren, November 20, 1837, Van Buren MSS.

script, receivable in payment of the public lands, in which a system of speculation was carried on by several registers and receivers, in a manner and under circumstances deserving the severest censure of the government and the people. The late register at Zanesville has been deeply implicated in these speculations and other malpractices. He was rebuked by the senate by the rejection of his nomination for his reappointment, and, with this exception, it is believed that the sales of public lands in Ohio, Indiana, Illinois, Missouri, and the Territory of Michigan are fairly made and according to the laws. The states of Alabama, Mississippi, and Louisiana have been the principal theater of speculation and fraud.[1]

In part, the substance of this report was correct; yet the land office correspondence of these and the following years discloses many abuses prevalent in the West. In September of 1835, the Galena, Illinois, and Lima, Ohio, offices had to be reprimanded for inefficiency; in May of the following year, Kalamazoo, Michigan, for permitting maps to be marked indicative of sales before the money was paid; in February of 1837, Fort Wayne, Indiana, for honest administration, but gross carelessness.[2]

Therefore the people of the West thought they had just cause in protesting against the methods employed in disposing of the public lands. The speculator with his ready cash, his advance knowledge of good lands acquired by shrewd agents, his connivance with the registers and the banks, and

[1] American State Papers, *Land*, VII, 733.

[2] *Registers and Receivers*, *New Series*, VI, September 17, 25, 1835; May 18, 1836; Amer. State Papers, *Land*, VII, 938–48.

the pressure he could bring to bear on the legislatures, had every advantage over the poor settler. The country people "waking or sleeping, eating or working" never thought of anything but land, and how to procure their equitable rights.[1] To them the whole land-office system was odious, and as they formed a large portion of the new states, they were able to turn the scale of public opinion in many an election when they united. Their protests had to be listened to; and it was to handle the evils of this situation and to appease these men that Jackson, in July of 1836, issued his famous Specie Circular.

The President's order was explained according to the political views of the interpreter. The Democrats said the Circular had been issued to stop the further monopolizing of the public land by speculators. So stated the last paragraph of the document, and so reiterated the *Washington Globe*, the official administration organ.[2] The Whigs naturally found entirely different reasons. The leading opposition papers united in their condemnation of the measure. They asserted its intent was to reduce the surplus, as the President at heart opposed the refunding of the people's money; that it enabled land speculators to sell their lands speedily at a handsome profit, so they might be able to refund the money they had borrowed from the pet banks; and that it aided the

[1] Hubbard to Van Buren, November 20, 1837, Van Buren MSS.
[2] *Globe*, July 21, 1836.

brokers, acting as agents "for some of the officers of the government, to realize fortunes for themselves and their employees by speculating in certificates of deposit signed by the United States treasurer, and transferable in whole or in part to land purchasers"; that western farmers would be compelled to buy their lands of the New York speculators "at a large advance, owing to the difficulty, and sometimes the impossibility, of procuring gold and silver"; that a panic would follow, but the election would be over, and what would the government care then for the settlers' distress and ruin? These charges were repeated innumerable times by the *Kennebec Journal*, the *Alton Telegraph*, the *Louisville Kentucky Journal*, the *Sangamon Journal*, the *St. Louis Republican*, the *Chicago American*, the *Ohio People's Press*, and other western papers.[1]

Whatever doubt there might be concerning the motives for the Specie Circular, the outcome of its operations were definite. Financial experts of today agree that the measure had a grievous effect on the money market.[2] The treasury order, by withdrawing specie from the East, and carrying it far into the interior, crippled the financial facilities of the former

[1] *Chicago American*, September 17, 1836; *Alton Telegraph*, April 12, 1837; *Sangamon Journal*, August 6, September 3, 1836; *St. Louis Republican, Louisville Kentucky Journal*, and others, quoted in the same papers.

[2] Sumner, *Jackson*, pp. 335–37; Wirth, *Geschichte der Handelkrisen*, p. 167.

area, while it led to a general contraction throughout the nation. The instant people saw that the
government suspected the reliability of the banking
institutions, "distrust seized upon the public mind,"
and "like fire in the great prairies," nothing could
stop it.[1] Specie began to disappear from circulation,
a fact that was confirmed even by good Democrats.
The money market was disturbed just as the banks
began to prepare to meet the demands of the distribution of the surplus. As these two forces began
to unsettle the business world, new demands came
from abroad, owing to the European situation. In
such an atmosphere, tense with uncertainty, the
Van Buren administration came into power.

The new President was besieged by his friends to
rescind the order. He was advised of the declining
strength of the past administration before its close,
and of the weakening effect upon his own if he continued to enforce the proclamation. The notion
which the West had received, that Van Buren was
not in favor of such measures as would benefit the
settlers, was probably one reason, as his friends
admitted, why he had not been stronger in the
West. He was urged to favor such bills as would
assist the settlers, if he hoped to make himself
popular in this section.[2] The statements of the

[1] *Cong. Globe, Twenty-fifth Cong., First Sess.*, p. 49.

[2] Skinner to Moses, January 3, 1837; Ward to Van Buren,
March 22, 1837; Boon to Van Buren, April 4, 1837; Lane to Van
Buren, May 27, 1837, Van Buren MSS.

Maysville Eagle, the *Cincinnati Republican*, and the utterances of men like Governor Duncan of Illinois were having a damaging influence on the party strength in the West.[1] The Democratic leaders in New York held a caucus and sent a special messenger to the President, urging upon him the necessity of repealing the act in order to establish the commercial confidence of the nation.[2] Whig politicians watched with anxiety the men in Washington, fearful lest the government would rescind the measure before the fall elections, and thus deprive the opposition of campaign material. Everything depended upon the firmness of the executive, and even Van Buren's friends trembled at this thought. Buchanan, writing to Jackson later on, expressed the universal belief among Democrats that the new President lacked stability.[3] If the order were repealed, it would discredit the Jacksonian administration; if it were retained it might cause even more distress. The only hope of the supporters of Jackson's policy was that the new administration was under a pledge to maintain the former's principles.

At last, on April 4, 1837, the *New York Journal of Commerce*, one of the leading Whig journals, gave

[1] *Maysville Eagle*, April 19, 1837; *Illinois Senate Journal* (1837), p. 8.

[2] Blatchford to Biddle, April 27, 1837. B.P.

[3] Buchanan to Jackson, July 28, 1837, Jackson MSS.

the public the information that the treasury order had not been repealed or released. It had been decided, so the paper declared, to adhere to the present policy, after a stormy meeting of the cabinet.

As a matter of fact, this report was misleading. Van Buren did not rescind the order, and he did not appeal to his cabinet for advice. At one time he did go so far as to draw up a series of questions to propound to the cabinet on the advisability of repeal, the public interest upon the subject, and the possible substitutes in place of the present measure. But he never submitted these questions, for, as he himself wrote, he decided to take the entire responsibility.

Van Buren's reasons for continuing the Specie Circular are found in a memorandum written by himself. They were as follows:

[(1) The repeal] would greatly increase the sale of public lands, and this would swell the surplus in the treasury. I have a letter from a gentleman at Jacksonville, Mississippi, dated February 28, stating that although the good lands in that district have been entered, the receipts at the land office there still amount to a thousand dollars a day, and such is the rage for speculation that nothing but want of money prevents every acre of public land from being taken up. The same rage for entering public land prevails throughout the country, it having been but imperfectly checked by the treasury circular. [(2) Repeal] would increase the surplus in the treasury—but it would exist as bank credit. [(3) Repeal] would add to the amount of notes in circulation. The whole amount of new bank credits thus created would exceed what would be paid for public lands. [4] Repeal of Specie Circular will cause specie to flow from the western states to the Atlantic states. The banks in the western states have not now, as appears from their recent returns, any more specie than is necessary to support the credit of their notes already in circulation. [5] Repeal would endanger the operation of paying over to the state the surplus funds in the treasury. . . . . If these surplus funds existed in the form of gold and silver, the operation of transferring them would be safe and easy. But they exist in the form of bank credits, and an attempt to transfer credits from one point to another frequently destroys it altogether. [6] Repeal would be only temporary. It would aid at first [the] New York banks. Then they would get money from the West—then enlarge their issues—then West would enlarge [their] issues, and soon conditions would be as bad as before. [7] Tendency of repeal . . . . to increase the mass of paper currency would not be effectually counteracted by the distrust the banks might have of each other. . . . . The constant tendency of banks, as N. Biddle has observed, "is to lend too much—to put too many notes in circulation." (All banks of West and Southwest would increase their notes if S.C. is repealed.) Banks of Mississippi, Louisiana, and Alabama . . . . appear to have run already the length of their tether. (New York would be aided temporarily as it got money from the West. But then it would [increase their] notes and cause trouble.)

Thus the repeal of the treasury circular would increase the paper currency throughout the Union; first, in the western states; secondly, in those parts of the Atlantic states from which large amounts of public funds are to be transferred; and thirdly, in those parts of the Atlantic states to which large amounts of public funds are to be transferred.

Lastly, supposing the banks in the southwestern states able to maintain their credit through the present crisis, it will increase the amount of paper medium even there. The currency of the other parts of the Union will then be more restricted (?) than that of the Southwest. The balance will be thrown in favor of the banks in that quarter, and they will extend their prices accordingly. [8] Any modification of the S.C. will produce these effects in proportion as it weakens the present operation of the Circular. The fault of the measure is (regarded from an economic point of view) not that it is too powerful, but that it is not powerful enough. In defiance of it, the banks in both the East and the West have increased their issues. To make the measure effective, according to its intent, it would be necessary to provide that the payments for the public lands should be *kept* in gold and silver, as well as made in gold and silver. [10] Repeal would aid. But—aid them to get gold from the West to New York, and thence to Liverpool.

At the same time Van Buren was resolved to maintain the Specie Circular, and was endeavoring to safeguard the interests of the westerner, Biddle was writing to Poinsett suggesting compromise proposals. Three days before the New York banks suspended, Biddle wrote Poinsett in the following strain:

I observe in the New York papers received this morning that the Specie Circular is not to be rescinded. It is idle to waste time in unavailing regrets, and I therefore have nothing more to say in regard to it, but it seems to me the next best thing would be a measure like this.

The Specie Circular is to be enforced—that is, the public lands are to be sold for gold and silver only. Be it so. But when it is deposited in the neighboring banks, it swells unnecessarily and perhaps dangerously the amount of public funds there, and it furnishes, moreover, an easy method of evading the rule by making the same parcel of specie perform the function of many land entries. Would it not be better to have these specie funds, exactly as they are received, deposited, not in the neighboring banks, but in the large deposit banks in the commercial cities? In this way (1) all the benefits proposed by the circular to repress speculation by a bona fide payment in specie would be secured. (2) The specie fund would be under the control of the treasury instead of being melted into the mass of credits due from the banks to the government. (3) This specie, taken from the commercial cities and wanted as the basis of circulation, will be thus restored to its proper function in the system of currency. I believe if such a measure were adopted and announced, so that the community would perceive that this element in the circulation was to be restored, it would revive confidence and produce an effect second only to what would be accomplished by the repeal itself.

This seems to be a sort of middle turn, in which all the forms of treasury order, and its substance, too, would be retained, while it would be disarmed of its practical inconvenience, the withdrawal from the currency of so large a portion of its defense.

If this idea strikes you favorably, I wish you would make it your own, and see if something might not be matured out of it.

The situation of the country requires that every man should contribute his share, however humble, to its relief—and you would not think I attach to it an exaggerated importance if you had the misfortune, as I have had, of mingling for the last six weeks with men who, sixty days ago, thought themselves beyond the reach of all the accidents of fortune, and find themselves and their families suddenly reduced to ruins.[1]

In these two statements we have the divergent views of the principal actors in the drama of the next few years. Van Buren was resolved to maintain the Specie Circular, and mistrusted the banks; Biddle was as equally determined to have it repealed, and was interested primarily in safeguarding the banks. If the banks were maintained, confidence would be restored, and the distress would have disappeared. So reasoned the financier.

Van Buren found himself confronted by the Philadelphian as the President took up the task left by his predecessor. Van Buren did not face the United States Bank, a national bank; but he did face the same organization, now a state bank, the United States Bank of Pennsylvania.

[1] Biddle to Poinsett, May 7, 1837, *President's Letter Books*.

CHAPTER III

BIDDLE AND THE RECHARTER
OF THE BANK

On the second day of March, 1836, one day before its charter had expired from the national government, the United States Bank accepted a charter from the state of Pennsylvania. Denied by the national administration the right to continue its operations, the president and directors of the Bank had applied for, and obtained, a grant from their own state; and thirteen days before the expiration of the old corporation, the "Bribery Bill," as the opponents called it, received the signature of Governor Ritner.[1] In less than three months Nicholas Biddle and his associates had managed to have had introduced and passed a bill to extend and renew the life of the institution. These had been trying months, both for the friends and for the foes of the measure, as a detailed study of the bill discloses.

The economic and political aspects of the state favored the Biddleites. Pennsylvania was already engulfed in the vast internal improvement speculation which characterized these years, and was just

[1] *Fifty-second Cong., Second Sess., Exec. Doc. 38*, Part I, S.N. 3059, p. 40.

beginning to feel the effects of her folly. With her commerce sinking beneath the pecuniary agitation of the thirties, and her citizens overburdened with taxes, the Pennsylvania Legislature was willing to listen to Nicholas Biddle.[1] Moreover, the Antimasonic party had elected their man, Joseph Ritner, as governor, upon an implied promise not to increase the debt or the taxes,[2] and as the Whigs and Antimasons had been voting together on all measures since 1832, under the able leadership of Thaddeus Stevens, the friends of the new bill deemed the time propitious.

The movement for recharter began in November of 1835. In the early part of the month Nicholas Biddle began to receive letters from friends, both within the state and in New York, advising him to petition the next session of the Pennsylvania Legislature, composed, as it was, of "flexible material."[3] New York seemed especially anxious for a charter, and therefore the Pennsylvania Legislature acted promptly.[4] By December 4, Biddle had a copy of the committees of the House, confidentially obtained "through the kindness of the speaker, Mr.

[1] *Harrisburg Chronicle*, May 30, 1836.

[2] McCarthy, "The Antimasonic Party," in *Amer. Hist. Assoc. Annual Report*, I, 461, 488.

[3] C. F. M. to Biddle, November 13, 1835; Morris to Biddle, November 16, 1835, B. P.

[4] Morris to Biddle, November 16, 1835, B.P.

Middlesworth, an old Antimasonic leader";[1] and on December 12, W. R. Reed, chairman of the Inland Navigation Committee, wrote that he considered it especially fortunate that a friend of the Bank had been placed at the head of the Internal Improvement Committee. "For," continued the writer, "the temptation of a turnpike, of a few miles of canal or railroad . . . . is nearly irresistible."[2] Therefore, when the chairman of the Ways and Means Committee, and the chairman of the Committee on Banks, on their own initiative and without the knowledge either of the House or their committees,[3] addressed a letter to Biddle asking him whether he would accept a charter from the state, and when Biddle, in reply, modestly declared the Bank was not opposed to becoming a state institution, provided the assembly acted before either New York, Maryland, New Jersey, or Delaware,[4] the opening skirmish in the struggle was concluded.

Notwithstanding the fact that Biddle presented the committee with an outline of a proposed char-

[1] McGrane, *Correspondence of Nicholas Biddle*, p. 257.

[2] *Op. cit.*, pp. 258–61. Cf. Reed's close relations with McIlvaine, McIlvaine to Biddle, January 16, 1836, B. P.

[3] Letter quoted in *New York Evening Post*, December 10, 1836; cf. also, *Report of the Select Committee Relative to the United States Bank, together with the Testimony Taken in Relation Thereto* p. 54 (Patterson, 1837) in the University of Pennsylvania Library.

[4] Biddle to Reed, December 18, 1835. *President's Letter Book*, V, 419–20.

ter, and that McIlvaine, Biddle's chargé at Harrisburg, kept in close touch with the friends of the Bank on the committee, three points caused trouble. The question of the size of the bonus, and the matter of state taxation were finally arranged to the satisfaction of both sides,[1] when Biddle suddenly heard that the governor and Thaddeus Stevens intended to introduce a provision that "if the Bank interfered with politics, its charter might be repealed," and another, "prohibiting the Bank from

---

[1] Biddle to Walker and Pennypacker, January 7, 1836, *P.L.B.*, V, 429, 432; Biddle to McIlvaine, January 7, 1836, *P.L.B.*, V, 426; *ibid.*, V, 427, 429; *Pennsylvanian*, January 22, 1836. Biddle had already presented some of the members of the committee with an outline of a proposed charter, according to which the new corporation, with a capital of $50,000,000, chartered for thirty years, would give $2,000,000 in cash to the state on the day it was incorporated, and, furthermore, would make liberal concessions to various internal improvement proposals. This outline was "susceptible of further compression," wrote Biddle to McIlvaine, but the latter was urged to call the attention of the friends of the measure to the sound reasons why the Bank ought to be rechartered by Pennsylvania. These were: (1) that Pennsylvania would thus become wealthy and surpass New York; (2) no fear of foreign capital, since many Europeans had already aided Pennsylvania in internal improvements; (3) Philadelphia had always been the seat of the Bank, and would become the center of finances if she rechartered the institution; (4) that New York's attacks were only designed to break down the Bank in Pennsylvania, in order to obtain one in New York; dissolution would mean the loss of $35,000,000, since foreign stockholders would not support a bank in which they had no confidence. Furthermore, the bill was first discussed only by the friends of the Bank in the committee, without the others being fully informed on the topic.

publishing documents." Biddle wrote immediately
to Reed and McIlvaine that this section must be
dropped, since, if "the Congress of the United
States could pass the bill in 1832 without annexing
such conditions, there was no reason why the Legislature of Pennsylvania should propose them, and
still less reason for one submitting to them."[1] As
restrictions they were unavailing, as indications of
opinion they were offensive,[2] and therefore must be
excluded, dictatorially demanded the president of
the Bank. This command, accompanied as it was
by a threat of withdrawing McIlvaine and seeking
other state legislatures, had the desired result, and
on January 18, Biddle was informed that the committee was ready to present a bill on the morrow
to the House, embodying the main ideas of the
adherents of the Bank.[3]

At last, on January 19, the recharter bill was
presented to the House. The title of the act of in-
corporation was unique. It was styled "An Act to
Repeal the State Tax on Real and Personal Property, and to Continue and Extend the Improvements of the State by Railroads and Canals; and to
Charter a State Bank to Be Called the United States
Bank."[4] In other words, the recharter articles,

[1] McGrane, *op. cit.*, p. 261; Biddle to McIlvaine, January 16,
1836, *P.L.B.*, V, 439, 441.

[2] *Ibid.*, pp. 261, 262.   [3] *Ibid.*, p. 262.

[4] *Journal of the House of Representatives*, I, 279, Harrisburg,
1835–36.

drawn up with consummate skill by those perfectly conversant with the subject,[1] appeared as clauses in a general appropriation measure. But this did not deceive the citizens of the state, or the nation at large. On January 5, the *Richmond Enquirer* called the attention of the people of Pennsylvania to the need of stability in the legislature on account of the devious maneuvers of the old bank.[2] The bank papers might remain silent on the topic, but the presence of the lobbyists at Harrisburg, and the fact that the stock had risen from 110 to 118 in a few days were signs that could not be mistaken.[3] Public meetings had been held for the purpose of proclaiming that the people had "no principles, to barter for gold,"[4] and everything had been done to arouse the populace to a sense of their duty. But it had been of no avail, for on the nineteenth of the month, the bank bill had been presented by the committees on inland navigation and internal improvements.

The bill proposed to make sundry improvements, and to incorporate the Bank of the United States with a capital of $28,000,000 for the consideration of a bonus of $2,000,000, to be appro-

[1] *American Sentinel*, January 25, 1836.

[2] *Richmond Enquirer*, January 5, 1836; *Pennsylvanian*, January 9, 1836.

[3] *Pennsylvanian*, January 15, 1836.

[4] *Ibid.*, January 15, 1836; January 18, 1836.

priated to various internal improvement schemes.[1]
Immediately a resolution was passed to refer to the
appropriate committees the different sections of the
bill,[2] and the friends and opponents of the Bank
began to prepare for the struggle. The Whigs and
Antimasons, as supporters of the institution, under
the able leadership of Thaddeus Stevens, were as
jealous of the Bank's rights as ever Queen Elizabeth
was of her prerogative.[3] Openly declaring that failure to recharter meant the distraction and destruction of the credit of the state, that New York would
become the center of finances and the end of the internal improvements, they urged its passage. The
opponents just as loudly called attention to the du-
ration of the new charter, the great capital of the new
corporation, and the manner in which the bill had
been drawn, in order "to gull the people by the
bribes offered . . . . in the shape of internal improvements."[4] Yet the friends of the measure never
doubted its final passage. Biddle was informed that
the bill would be amended in the House by Stevens,
but that "our friends were sanguine of its success,"[5]

[1] *Pennsylvanian*, January 22, 1836; *American Sentinel*, January 21, 1836.

[2] *Ibid.*, January 20, 1836.

[3] Shunk to Buchanan, January 21, 1837, in Buchanan MSS,
in Pennsylvania Historical Society Library. These arguments in
1837 were similar to those employed in 1836 in Pennsylvania.

[4] *American Sentinel*, January 21, February 18, 1836.

[5] Cowperthwait to Biddle, January 21, 1836, B.P.

and so it was amended. Certain clauses on internal improvements were stricken out, the Bank was required to pay $100,000 for seven years to the school fund, and to pay a bonus of $4,500,000, with the privilege of paying $2,000,000 of the said bonus within twenty years.[1] Biddle might groan at the action of Stevens in introducing the bonus increase, comparing himself to Isaac the Jew in the castle of Front-de-Boeuf, but when the second reading passed by a vote of fifty-one to thirty-three, his pangs were mollified. The vote in the House was nearly a party vote—all the Antimasons and Whigs, with one or two exceptions, voting for the bill, and the Democrats against it.[2] In truth, few obstacles were placed in the path of the friends of the Bank. Except for the slight inconveniences caused by the Antimasonic investigation, which for a while delayed its motion, or when "the young members of the House had engagements to go sleighing with the ladies" and refused to be distracted, or when McIlvaine had to convince Stevens that Biddle was a "beggared and bankrupt man," from whom neither fire nor rack could extort another denier; or when the governor showed signs of opposing its enactment, the fight in the House was uneventful.[3]

[1] *Pennsylvanian*, January 29, 1836.

[2] *American Sentinel*, January 29, 1836.

[3] Wallace to Biddle, January 19, 1836; Chandler to Biddle, January 21, 1836; Cowperthwait to Biddle, January 21, 1836;

Thus, when the members of the assembly, after a disgraceful scramble to get portions of the bonus for their specific internal improvements, passed the bill by a vote of fifty-seven to thirty, the first stage of the contest was over. On the third reading there were thirteen members absent. One Democrat voted for the bill, and one Whig and one Antimason against it.[1]

The action of the House aroused the opponents of the measure to even greater exertions. The newspapers of the state resolved to appeal to the people over the heads of their representatives,[2] and the arguments they employed contain many of the cogent phrases of the political philosophy of the ancient régime. "All power is inherent in the people," boldly proclaimed the *Pennsylvanian*, on January 29. Therefore, if the aristocratic legislature should incorporate the Bank and thrust reform aside, the people, "resolving the community into its original elements," might elect delegates to frame a new constitution for their government, and "begin their political existence *de novo*." The names of

---

Wallace to Biddle, January 22, 1836, January 23, 1836; McIlvaine to Biddle, January 26 (?), 1836, B.P. The friends of the Bank were also afraid to rush the recharter measure, for fear "those members whose bills were postponed might vote against this bill which was preferred to theirs."

[1] *American Sentinel*, February 2, 1836.

[2] *Globe*, February 3, 1836; *American Sentinel*, January 29, 1836.

some of the foreign stockholders in the Bank were likewise published in order to arouse the citizens, while great stress was laid on the dictatorial manner in which Thaddeus Stevens had corralled votes for the institution.[1] But the friends of Biddle were undaunted by these assaults. The fact that Maryland and New York were anxiously seeking the capital of the old bank led them to make a determined stand.[2] Therefore, when the fight was shifted to the Senate, many of the friends of the Bank openly boasted that they had secured seven of the Democratic senators, three of whom had a double part to play: they were to vote against the bill, if it should be carried without them, in order to save their places with the Democracy, and in order to serve the Bank hereafter; but, if the charter could not be carried without their votes, they were to vote for it at all hazards.[3]

However, the friends of the bill were not, and, in truth, had never been, confident of the Senate.

[1] *Pittsburg Gazette*, quoted in *American Sentinel*, January 30, 1836.

[2] Niles, January 30, 1836; the Biddle papers contain many letters from friends in Maryland asking the Bank to petition for a charter in their state; and although Biddle did not follow up this suggestion at the present, he declared if the governor did "not sign the bill, to consider Maryland." The fact that he had already petitioned Pennsylvania, and as time progressed he saw the successful culmination of his efforts, deterred him from immediate action, but throughout the fight in the Senate, Biddle used this outside pressure to good advantage.

[3] *Globe*, February 3, 1836; *American Sentinel*, February 4, 1836.

From the beginning of the controversy this branch
had been a source of anxiety, and was conceded to
be doubtful, but, undaunted, McIlvaine and his
cohorts set to work interesting the committees as
they had done in the House. Senators Dickey and
Penrose were consulted by the private agent of
Biddle, and the method of introducing the bill was
soon arranged. The chief difficulty in the committee stage centered around the determination of
Dickey to have a branch in Beaver County. This,
the noble senator declared, was his *sine qua non*, as
it was the only possible excuse he could offer his
constituents for his vote.[1] McIlvaine acknowledged
the justice of the senator's contention, especially as
the latter threatened to vote against the bill, and
carry two other votes with him.[2] Biddle, in reply to
a request for advice from his chargé, stated that he
was not opposed to a branch at Beaver, but to the
naming of a branch anywhere, which might lead to
the naming of others, and finally to the destruction
of the bill itself.[3] Still, if the senator insisted upon
it, Biddle was willing to agree.

Finally, on January 30, the bill was introduced
in the Senate. As friends in Maryland were constantly urging Biddle to apply to their state if the
Senate refused to pass the bill, or hesitated over the

[1] Wallace to Biddle, February 1, 1836, B.P.
[2] McIlvaine to Biddle, January 30 (?), 1836, B.P.
[3] Biddle to McIlvaine, January 31, 1836, B.P.

terms, the bank men were insistent upon haste. "As the troops were raw, they could not be brought into action," wrote one senator to Biddle on February 5, but a "council of war had been held, and it had been decided to force matters."[1] Accordingly, the adherents of the measure brought a test vote on the question of taking up the bill. This resulted in twenty-one ayes against twelve nays, and the Whigs boasted that this vote was prophetic of the final count, as it ultimately proved to be.[2] The enemy appeared crestfallen; even their leader admitting that he did not think it was worth fighting strenuously, while others intimated they might like to vote favorably, but for fear they would be "tarred and feathered."[3] Nevertheless, McIlvaine knew that the fight was not over, and although he and his followers endeavored to work without delay, the opposing side continued to present as many obstacles as possible in their path. The hotels and lobbies were thronged with the supporters of the measure.[4]

On February 9, the *Daily Reporter* and the *Journal* published an account of an attempt to bribe one of the senators. When called before the bar of the Senate, the junior editor acknowledged

[1] McGrane, *op. cit.*, p. 264.

[2] Wallace to Biddle, February 5, 1836, B.P. The price of a share in the Bank rose to 126 at this time (Niles, February 6, 1836).

[3] Wood to Beban, February 7, 1836, B.P.

[4] McIlvaine to Biddle, February 8, 1836, B.P. Cf. newspapers of the same date.

that he had written the article on hearsay information, implicating Colonel Krebs, senator from Schuylkill County.[1] The Colonel, when called upon to answer these charges before the Senate, made the following dramatic speech:

On January 28, declared Krebs, James L. Dunn called upon me and stated that he had some coal lands which he could sell for eight or ten thousand dollars more if this bill to recharter the Bank of the United States would pass, and if I would vote for it, he would give me one-half of the sum. . . . . I told him I could agree to no such proposition. . . . . After the bill was brought into the senate, H. W. Conrad, representative from Schuylkill County, told me that if I voted for the bill . . . . that Burd Patterson of the same county would make arrangements with me that I should get twenty thousand dollars for my vote within two weeks after the bill became a law. I told Conrad that poor as I was, the Bank of the United States had not enough money to buy my vote.[2]

Immediately committees were appointed in both branches to investigate the bribery charges. Two friends of the bill and three opponents composed the Senate committee, and three Whigs and two Democrats, the House committee.[3]

[1] *National Gazette*, February 16, 1836. A member of Perry County, and Colonel Crabbe, editor of *Carlisle Republican*, gave the information.

[2] *Pennsylvanian*, February 13, 1836.

[3] *American Sentinel*, February 15, 1836; Niles, February 20, 1836; *Pennsylvanian*, February 13, 1836. (Conrad had the reputation of being a practical joker.)

Both committees set to work collecting information. The Senate committee asked leave from
the House to interrogate Conrad, and after examin-
ing the other principals in the case, made its final
report on the fifteenth. The evidence disclosed the
fact that Patterson had not approached Krebs
directly, but indirectly through Conrad; that the
former had authorized Conrad to request Krebs to
offer an amendment to the bill to get an appropriation to the Danville and Pottsville Railroad; but
Patterson denied that Krebs had been told "he
might retire to private life, independent, if he voted
for the measure."[1] Therefore the committee reported that they were perfectly convinced that
neither the Bank of the United States nor any
agent of it were either implicated in the charge of
bribery, or had improperly interfered to promote its
passage.[2]

The House committee did not render its final
decision until two months after the bill had become
a law. Nevertheless, the conclusions it set forth
were more complete and more detailed. The committee branded as fabrication the story of Conrad's
attempt to bribe Krebs at Patterson's suggestion;
and then it proceeded to analyze the motives of the
various actors. The fact that Conrad had made his

[1] *American Sentinel*, February 15, 1836; *National Gazette*,
February 18, 1836.

[2] *Pennsylvanian*, February 18, 1836.

statement to Krebs in a barroom, and in a loud voice in the presence of many hearers, marked the attempt as a joke. Moreover, the fact that Colonel Krebs did not report the occurrence to the Senate for ten days, and then only after a vague rumor of its existence, proved that the Colonel had not taken the words of Conrad seriously. Therefore the committee declared the whole affair was a "deliberate plan concocted beyond the limits of Pennsylvania," and, as the committee viewed the situation, Colonel Krebs had written a private letter to his friends in Schuylkill County, which he hoped they would make public, intimating that he had been approached by bank men. Furthermore, Conrad had likewise visited the same county, and in order to stir up the populace, had circulated similar reports regarding attempts at bribery in connection with himself and Colonel Krebs. But, when the latter was called upon by the Senate to answer these charges, Krebs "took advantage of the casual remarks of Conrad to shelter himself, while Conrad, finding himself charged with being the author as well as the propagator of the slander, endeavored to divert public indignation from himself and fix it upon another by boldly maintaining the reality of the corrupt proposition." Thus the committee[1] reit-

---

[1] Report quoted in full in Niles, April 9, 1836. Cf. letters of Krebs to Trailey, February 4, 1836 in *Record of the Testimony, Proceedings and Reports of the Committee . . . . to Inquire into*

erated their belief that the whole affair had been a plot conceived beyond the state, and accordingly recommended that Conrad be reprimanded for his actions.

Therefore in both reports the Bank was vindicated of all direct attempts at bribery. Throughout the whole episode, the correspondence of the agents of the Bank to Biddle had taken about the same stand as that of the House committee. McIlvaine, writing on February 5, stigmatized the affair of old Krebs as a "humbug"; Todd described the case as "all smoke"; while Wallace wrote that he was unable to determine whether Krebs was "so utterly stupid as not to understand the meaning and nature of a bribe, or so wicked as to pervert innocent conversations to political profit."[1]

The Bank was not, however, materially interrupted by the bribery scandal, although the stock

---

the Attempt of Henry W. Conrad, Esquire . . . . to Influence and Bribe the Vote of Jacob Krebs (Harrisburg, 1836), pp. 40, 41. Found in the University of Pennsylvania Library.

[1] McIlvaine to Biddle, February 15, 1836; Todd to Biddle, February 13, 1836; Wallace to Biddle, February 13, 1836, B.P. The following is on p. 182 of the *Report of the Testimony given before the Joint Committee of Investigation*, inquiring into the charges whether any corrupt means had been used by the banks to obtain favorable legislation from 1836 to 1840: "In regard to the recharter of the Bank of the United States, some evidence, however, was incidentally brought before the committee, from which it would seem scarcely to be doubted that the same means were attempted, if not actually employed, at that time, as during

in Philadelphia fell from 129½ to 126.[1] Undisturbed by the conditions in the Senate, or the public attitude without, Biddle and McIlvaine pressed the friendly senators to an aggressive policy, and accordingly, on the fifteenth, the bill passed the third reading by a vote of nineteen to twelve, which McIlvaine had prophesied to Biddle some time before

the session of 1840. The permanent expense account of that bank before referred to shows the following entries during the year 1836:

May 5, Receipt of N. Biddle, president	$20,575.00
May 7, Receipt of N. Biddle, president	5,000.00
May 16, Voucher for incidental expenses at Harrisburg	1,311.00
May 23, Receipt of N. Biddle	8,697.50
May 23, John B. Wallace, for professional services	10,000.00
May 23, Joseph McIlvaine, for professional services	10,000.00
May 27, N. Biddle	10,000.00
June 13, N. Biddle	5,000.00
June 24, M. Wilson & Co., Harrisburg, for expenses	3,468.50
June 10, N. Biddle	5,000.00
	$79,052.00

"How many more of the items of the same account entered as of a subsequent date refer back to the transaction in question, the committee cannot determine. They call attention, however, to the evidence of Jonathan Patterson, one of the tellers of the Bank, who proves the use of the sum of $400,000 by the officers, at or about the very period of the recharter, the withdrawal of which from the Bank was attempted to be concealed by a false entry on the books. Both of the agents who appear to have been employed on this occasion are now deceased, and to have proceeded further in such an investigation, without having the time to prosecute it to its full extent, did not seem to be proper under the circumstances." App. to Vol. II, *Fifty-second Sess. House of Representatives of . . . . Pennsylvania* (1842), p. 182.

[1] *Pennsylvanian*, February 17, 1836.

would be the final vote. Only one Whig, Mr. Baker, voted against its passage, and he published an open letter explaining his position.[1] The bill was then sent to the House, and on the sixteenth the latter branch agreed to the Senate's amendments.

Governor Ritner was now called upon to decide a question pregnant with consequences to himself, his state, and his friends. The fear of offending his party and of displeasing the people, together with the mixed character of the bill upon which he was called to give his decision, rendered his high office anything but a sinecure. Although in former years he had favored the recharter of the Bank by the national government, and a liberal system of internal improvements, his position on the present measure had been an enigma alike to friend and foe. Within late years, his messages and speeches on the policy of internal improvements had cautioned moderation,[2] and this, for a while, boded ill for the present measure with its extravagant provisions. But, as time progressed, McIlvaine and others at Harrisburg assured Biddle, the governor would sign the bill. As Todd declared to Biddle, Ritner was a Pennsylvanian,[3] and as he wanted to aid his state and check Van Buren, there was no cause for alarm. Moreover, Thaddeus Stevens, the

[1] *Pennsylvanian*, February 26, 1836.
[2] McCarthy, *op. cit.*, pp. 446, 472.
[3] Todd to Biddle, February 3, 1836, B.P.

acknowledged leader of the Antimasonic party, was working on the government, and as Ritner "looked upon his election as a triumph of Antimasonry," the chief magistrate was not likely to oppose Stevens or his friends—either Whig or Antimason.[1] The people soon began to apprehend that there was no hope in this quarter, for, as the *American Sentinel* of February 17 remarked, Governor Ritner did not have enough "Snyder" in him to veto the bill. The state was not greatly surprised accordingly, when, on the eighteenth, the bill received his signature.

At last the great "Bribery Bill of Pennsylvania" had passed into law, owing largely to the able generalship of Nicholas Biddle and Joseph McIlvaine. By working on the committees, by offering the members of the legislature liberal grants in the form of internal improvement provisions, and by constantly holding over the assembly the threat of seeking aid elsewhere, they outgeneraled the Democrats. From all sides Nicholas Biddle received the congratulations and plaudits of his friends.[2] The stock of the Bank rose from 125 to 129 in less than

[1] Wallace to Biddle, February 6, 7, 11, 14, 1836, B.P.; McCarthy, *op. cit.*, p. 473.

[2] The stock of the Bank of the United States, when it accepted the charter from Pennsylvania, was as follows: "To the New England states, $3,111,000; New York and New Jersey, $4,569,000; Delaware, Maryland, and the District of Columbia, $2,027,000; Virginia and North Carolina, $894,000; South Carolina and Georgia, $3,031,000; other states, $99,000; Pennsylvania, $5,219,000; foreigners. . . . ." *P.L.B.* (1836), p. 136.

a week, and property in Erie, Pennsylvania, doubled in value.[1] In the United States Senate, Ewing of Ohio triumphantly proclaimed the recharter, while Calhoun renewed his attacks on the administration.[2] But the opponents of the old United States Bank did not falter in their opposition. Crestfallen in Pennsylvania, they were spurred on by the actions of neighboring states. The Ohio Legislature passed a bill prohibiting the establishment of agencies or branches in that state, much to the surprise and alarm of Biddle and his friends.[3] Rumors were likewise circulated regarding the supposed antagonism of Virginia and New York.[4] Even President Jackson contemplated action against the bill when drafting the Specie Circular.[5] Signs of discord

[1] Biddle to Bowers, February 24, 1836, *P.L.B.*, V, 482; Russell to Buchler, February 28, 1836, in Wolf MSS.

[2] *Globe*, quoted in *Pennsylvanian*, February 19, 1836.

[3] *Pennsylvanian*, March 25, 1836; Penrose to Biddle, March 26, 1836; Trevor to Biddle, March 24, 1836, B.P.

[4] *Pennsylvanian*, February 24, 1836.

[5] In a memorandum containing an addition to the treasury circular, the following was appended: "And whereas the Bank of the United States seized upon a large sum . . . . belonging to the people, which up to this time had been withheld from them and from their use, and it has declined to give any satisfactory information respecting the seven millions of stock belonging to the public in its capital; and whereas the whole assets of the Bank, including the part belonging to the government and the people, have been transferred over to the individual stockholders in the Bank, who have been incorporated by an act of the Legislature of the State of Pennsylvania under the same name, and the

began to appear on all sides. The old alliance of
Whigs and Antimasons began to dissolve, and a new
party, headed by such men as Dr. Burden, Dickey,
and others, calling themselves the "States' Right
Party," favoring Webster for president, made its
appearance in Pennsylvania.[1] The Democratic
prints urged the people to frame a new constitution in order to check the Bank, and at the fall election, only eight of the representatives who had composed a majority on the recharter were rechosen.[2]
But Nicholas Biddle, who had so successfully
maneuvered the bank bill through the legislature,
from its earliest conception to its final passage, was
still in control of affairs, and under the name of the
United States Bank of Pennsylvania the old corporation started on a new career, soon to succumb
to the economic effects of the panic of 1837.

---

whole seven millions of the public fund of the public money
which formed a part of the capital of the late Bank of the United
States, as well as the sum which has been withheld of the public
dividends, have been appropriated to the use of the said individual
stockholders, notice is also hereby given that until a full and satisfactory settlement is made for the said seven millions which the
people had in the capital of the Bank, and a full restitution of the
sum withheld of the public dividend, no notes whatever issued by
the Bank of the United States will be received in payment of any
public dues." This was indorsed by Jackson, "to be considered as
to the present or future time" (Jackson MSS).

[1] *Pennsylvanian*, March 8, 10, 1836.

[2] *Ibid.*, February 25, 26, 1836; *Plain Dealer*, December 3, 1836.

CHAPTER IV

FINANCIAL AND INDUSTRIAL
ASPECTS OF THE PANIC

First, in order of time as well as of importance, of the long train of events that prepared the way for the panic of 1837, was the destruction of the United States Bank, and the subsequent removal of deposits. The banks selected to receive these governmental funds immediately began to extend their loans; while the hope of obtaining a portion of the deposits led to the creation of hundreds of new banks. Merchants were tempted and invited to borrow from the banks in order to enlarge their business operations. The value of all kinds of property rose to fabulous heights. Men of limited resources, in their mad haste to be rich, bought land, city lots, and stocks. A restless spirit of adventure and daring enterprise swept the nation. Over-trading, speculation, and investments in unproductive undertakings became the dominant note in American society. The sales of public lands outstripped the wildest expectations; and as our nation paid off its debt, and began to pile up a surplus in the treasury, largely as the result of the sales of the public domain, our credit was expanded to maintain the

overaction in trading. When such credit could not
be secured here, the American people were confident it could be obtained abroad. Thus a large
foreign indebtedness was incurred at a time when
our imports were exceeding our exports.

But this state of unnatural and delusive prosperity could not always last. The act for the distribution of the surplus revenue became law in
June of 1836. This was quickly followed by the
treasury's order transferring the public money from
points where it was collected to other places, in
anticipation of its distribution among the states.
On July 11, 1836, to curb the speculative actions in
connection with the land sales, the Specie Circular
was issued, by which gold and silver were made
receivable for public lands. The effect of these two
later measures was to transfer "by a forced and
most unnatural process, a considerable portion of
the public moneys, and a large amount of specie
from the Atlantic cities to the western states."
Utter confusion was introduced into the nation's
monetary affairs, and confidence was weakened.
The government made the most unreasoning demands upon the deposit banks. They, in turn, were
compelled to call upon their customers. At the
same time there was a crop shortage, due to the
devastating effects of the Hessian fly. The next
spring found the merchants pressed by the banks
and by their foreign creditors. All the banks were

driven to the necessity of a rapid curtailment of their business. Money, from having been abundant, became increasingly scarce. On May 10, 1837, the New York banks suspended specie payment. The following days the banks of Philadelphia, Baltimore, Albany, Hartford, New Haven, and Providence suspended payment; on the twelfth, the banks of Mobile and New Orleans; on the fifteenth, the District of Columbia banks; Charleston and Cincinnati on the seventeenth; and on the nineteenth, the Louisville and Augusta banks closed their doors.[1]

Contemporary opinion gave various reasons for the collapse of credit. The more unsophisticated found the explanation in the consequences of the extensive conflagration in the city of New York in December, 1835, which destroyed twenty million dollars' worth of property; but as a rule the general inferences were tinged with the political views of the interpreter. By some the derangements in the domestic exchanges were credited to the destruction of the United States Bank; to others the accumulation and distribution of the surplus revenue by the

[1] Good general accounts of the background of the crisis can be found in Governor Marcy's message of January 2, 1838, in *New York Senate Journal, Sixty-first Sess.* (1838), pp. 9–12; *Votes and Proceedings of Sixty-second General Assembly, New Jersey* (1837), pp. 55–58; account of business men's convention on causes in *N.Y. Journal of Commerce*, August 9, 1837. On crop failures of 1836, cf. *Maysville Eagle*, June 11, July 2, 1836; Niles, July 23, 1836.

administration were the sources of the present distress; by others it was attributed to the Specie Circular, while still another class found it in the overtrading and speculation which had raged for the
last three years among all classes and in all industrial activities. But all agreed in condemning the
banks for their immediate suspension of specie
payments, and calling upon the bankers to justify
their actions.[1]

This justification was offered by Biddle in a
letter to a committee of the citizens of Philadelphia on May 18:

> The suspension of specie payments by the United States
> Bank was occasioned by this—that the government of the
> United States first stopped paying specie to the citizens of
> Philadelphia—and that the bankers of New York stopped
> paying specie to the citizens of Philadelphia. The banks of
> Philadelphia therefore thought if others would not pay specie
> to them and to the citizens of Philadelphia, it would be wrong
> of them to pay specie to others, because this would be paying
> specie at the expense of the citizens of Philadelphia. The
> specie in the banks of Philadelphia is the funds on which
> loans are made to the merchants, manufacturers, and
> mechanics of Philadelphia. When the specie diminishes, the
> loans are diminished, and if the banks had gone on paying
> specie to the government and to the New York banks, they
> would have been obliged to cease lending to the merchants,
> manufacturers, and mechanics—and the consequence would
> be that all the laboring classes employed by them would

[1] *Exec. Doc., Twenty-fifth Cong., Second Sess.*, Vol. IV, No. 79,
pp. 8, 10, 11.

have been turned out of employment. If the banks part with their specie, they must stop lending. The simple question, then, was whether to suspend the factories—suspend all trade, suspend all house-building, all canal-making, all road-making—or to suspend specie payment. . . . . If the banks had been so thoughtless as to go on till all the specie had been drawn from them, how could they lend money to pay the wages of the industrious classes, who would have been thrown out of employment by thousands?

Then the bank president launched into a long defense of the moneyed institutions.

There is a notion abroad that the banks are unfavorable to the laboring classes. This is a very great mistake. The best friends of the laboring classes are the banks; what laboring people want is labor, work, constant employment. How can they get it? In building shops and in building houses; in coal mines; in making roads and canals; and how are all these carried on except by credit in the shape of loans from banks. If it were not from such credits, nine-tenths of all the works which give wages to labor would be at an end.

Banks may sometimes be badly managed, as everything else in the world may be, but good banks are the great support of industry. If there was nothing but gold and silver in the country, the banks would be limited to what could be paid by gold and silver, and the owners of gold and silver would be the only persons who could employ workmen; so that all men who had nothing but their industry to depend on could have no chance of getting up in the world. It is the banks who give them credit to enable them to rise. The greatest misfortune to the laboring classes would be to banish the system of credit. In fact, the present troubles are mainly owing to the absurd attempt to force gold and silver into circulation. Gold and silver are for the rich—safe bank-notes are the democracy of currency. The laboring classes ought therefore to stand by the banks as their best friends.[1]

The banker's defense was lost upon the masses struggling for existence in the midst of economic chaos. With factories and workshops closing down; with business failures occurring in astounding rapidity; and with appeals for help from all sides, the philosophical discussion of the Philadelphia financier was ignored in the practical emergencies of the day; and how great these difficulties were can be seen by describing the industrial condition of each section during the next few years.

No adequate appreciation of the devastation wrought in the East can be acquired without paying especial attention to New York City and New York State. As was set forth in a former chapter New York City was the vortex and center of the prosperity of the country between 1830 and 1836. She represented the East, and the nation in all its aspects, and now she was to show in like manner the vicissitudes of all the sections. By June of 1836, Biddle was informed of the nervousness apparent among the deposit banks, by the needs of the distribution act. They were cautious and circumspect in their policy, in view of the public demands about to be placed upon them.[2] The close of the year found matters worse, and by March of 1837, failures

[1] Biddle to Committee, May 18, 1837, B.P.

[2] Davis to Biddle, June 23, 1836, B.P.

among business houses were common occurrences. Merchants who had traded on a large scale with the Southwest found their notes coming back to them, thereby forcing some of the most substantial houses to fail, suspend, or ask for time. There was a prospect, however, that the banks might be able to sustain the pressure, if the exposure of frauds committed, with the connivance of some of their officers, on the Mechanics' and Dry Dock banks, and the excitement caused by that disclosure and by the sudden death of the president of the Mechanics' Bank had not unnerved the entire community.[1] On May 9, $652,000 in specie was withdrawn from the vaults of the city banks; and on the evening of the same day it was learned that the principal deposit banks could not sustain themselves, as they had fewer funds than other institutions, while some of the local banks had but a few thousand dollars.[2] The next day the banks of New York suspended payment.[3] This was, for the moment, approved, because it actually involved an abrogation of debts, thereby enabling every debtor to settle his accounts at a discount of 8 to 10 per cent.[4] But it entailed,

[1] *Senate Doc., Twenty-fifth Cong., Second Sess.*, Vol. IV, Doc. 365, pp. 20, 21, Report from Sec. of Treasury, ... transmitting the replies of the deposit banks.

[2] *Ibid.*, p. 29.

[3] Cambreleng to Van Buren, May 10, 1837, Van Buren MSS.

[4] *Senate Doc., Twenty-fifth Cong., Second Sess.*, Vol. IV, No. 365, p. 24.

at the same time, a general suspension of business. A perfect apathy settled over the community. Barges and tow boats lay idle at the docks, building operations ceased, and thousands of laborers were thrown out of employment.[1]

Throughout the summer and fall this condition of affairs remained about the same. At times the pressure was a little more severe, at times less. Meanwhile, the air of despondency and lack of confidence were the prevailing notes of the market. Nevertheless, with the exception of those descriptions of property the value of which was entirely, or in a great degree, imaginary, prices could scarcely be said to have been unfavorably affected, "at least not so universally as to indicate a depreciation of the currency. Although during most of the time bank notes, as compared with specie, were depreciated about 5 per cent, no corresponding effect upon prices was apparent," and when, in 1838, resumption took place in New York, "prices, if anything, seemed rather to advance." The New York bank commissioners in 1839, in commenting on the condition, declared it was the only instance of a general suspension they knew of "unattended by a visible fluctuation in the prices of property generally, and we think it shows that much of the evil which legitimately follows such a calamity may be averted by judicious measures properly

[1] Davis to Biddle, June 2, 1837, B.P.

applied in season." They attributed the mitigation of the evil in this instance "to the rapid and steady curtailment pursued by the banks; to the sound condition of the agricultural interest at the time of the suspension, and to the general confidence inspired by these and other circumstances in the ability of the banks to effect a speedy resumption."[1]

The suspension of specie payment by the banks was followed by the disappearance of coin as a circulating medium. As specie was at a premium, it was hoarded by those who possessed it, and to carry on necessary business transactions, small bills became the medium of exchange. The New York banks were prohibited from issuing these notes by a law passed in 1835 by the legislature, endeavoring to further the government's efforts to infuse a larger portion of the precious metals into the channels of trade. With the suspension of specie payments, these notes flowed in from the surrounding states until their amount, below the denomination of five dollars, was estimated, by 1838, at from three to four million dollars. But it was not alone their amount, or the consequent loss to the citizens of the state, as a community, of the interest upon them, which constituted the greatest objection to their use. Many of them were spurious; many were the issue of expired or broken institutions, or of

[1] *New York Assembly Doc., Sixty-second Sess.* (1839), Vol. III, No. 101, pp. 3, 4, Bank Commissioner's Report.

insolvent corporations.[1] To remedy this situation
the legislature in February, 1838, permitted the
banks to circulate small bills.[2] At the same time
the banks curtailed their loans and discounts, increased their specie, and in defiance of Biddle's protest resumed specie payments in May, 1838. This
was followed by a slight revival of trade, but
throughout the year business was unsettled, due to
the general condition of the country, and the political agitation over the sub-treasury in Congress.

Another reason for the slight improvement in
the business outlook was the enactment of a new
banking law in 1838. Governor Marcy, in his message to the legislature in January, 1838, commented
at length on the financial situation. Referring to
the special privileges possessed by the banks, and
the current opinion that these privileges created a
monopoly, he said: "To obviate this objection, it is
desirable to discontinue the present mode of granting charters, and to open the business of banking to
a full and free competition under such general
restrictions and regulations as are necessary to
insure to the public at large a sound currency."
This he believed could best be secured by pressing a
general banking law. The legislature adopted the
governor's suggestion. The new law authorized
the comptroller to cause to have engraved and

---

[1] *New York Senate Doc., Sixty-first Sess.* (1838), I, 1, 2.

[2] *New York Laws* (1838), pp. 26–28.

printed circulating notes "in the similitude of bank notes in blank" which were issued at his office. Banking associations were allowed to exchange state or federal stock for an equal amount of these circulating notes, and such banking associations might thereupon issue the circulating notes "as money," according to banking usages.

Provision was made for protesting these notes for nonpayment by the bank on demand, and for their payment by the comptroller out of the trust funds deposited with him by the bank. Banking associations, instead of depositing public stocks, might deliver to the comptroller bonds and mortgages on real estate for the half of the value of the circulating notes to be taken. Persons desiring to form a banking association were authorized to make a certificate stating the required facts and record it in the office of the secretary of state. This authorized the association to enjoy the benefits of the law and procure from the comptroller circulating notes with which to carry out its business. The association was required to keep on hand specie to the amount of at least $12\frac{1}{2}$ per cent of its circulating notes.[1]

At the same time the legislature passed laws extending the time limit for insolvent insurance companies, dealt drastically with fraudulent debtors, and gave relief to partnerships.[2] These acts undoubtedly increased the morale of business, and as Governor Seward stated in 1841, currency was especially aided by the free-banking laws of 1838.[3]

---

[1] Lincoln, *The Constitutional History of New York*, II, 42, 43.

[2] *New York Laws* (1838), pp. 21, 22, 97, 243, 244.

[3] Lincoln, *op. cit.*, II, pp. 42, 43.

The slight reversal at the close of 1838 stimulated false hopes. The governor's message of 1839 asserted that the gloom which had spread over the country "had passed away."[1] His statement was a little premature. There had been a partial alleviation of the pressure, but the evil had not been removed. Nevertheless, the people took it for granted that the past was gone forever, and acting on their former policy began to speculate. With the retirement of Biddle as president of the United States Bank of Pennsylvania, the old corporation became involved in cotton manipulations. Other institutions and individuals likewise indulged their whims, with the result that at the close of the year the nation was once more engulfed in the throes of a financial crisis. The result is well known. For obvious reasons, the merchants had not been able to act so extravagantly as in the years preceding the great crisis. Accordingly, New York weathered the flurry with more ease. But in order to further regulate the banking processes, the legislature enacted the following year a law requiring corporations "to designate an agent with an office in New York or Albany to honor all bills of banking associations which might be presented for redemption, and it was made the duty of such agent to redeem such bills on presentation and demand." This law, together with the former free-banking act, and the

[1] Baker, editor, *Works of W. H. Seward*, II, 183.

one restoring the circulation of small bills, in the
opinion of Governor Seward finally restored the
banking institutions to their old position of security.[1] But the panic of 1837 had left deep scars on the
financial and commercial districts of the city and
state of New York, and for five years (1837–42)
New York City struggled to overcome the avalanche
she had been preparing against herself from 1830
to 1836.

In the meantime, the internal improvements of
New York had been grievously affected by the stringency. It will be recalled that New York, Pennsylvania, and various other eastern states had pushed
the internal improvement policy with much vigor
during the years of inflated currency. It was not
surprising, therefore, when the panic came, that
these projects were caught in the whirlwind. Governor Marcy, in reviewing the situation of the New
York canals during 1837, admitted a falling off of
$275,000 in tolls in consequence of the scanty crops
of 1836 and the diminished westward trade;[2] but undaunted by this loss, the governor asked for a still
larger appropriation. Governor Seward, in his annual message, favored the idea of retrenchment,
while at the same time expressing a hope that the
Erie Canal, which was in particular difficulty, would
be pushed forward with as much energy as the cir-

[1] Lincoln, *op. cit.*, II, pp. 42, 43.

[2] Whitford, *History of the Canal System of New York*, I, 160.

cumstances would allow. Notwithstanding the
sound advice given by Governor Seward and Comptroller Flagg, the legislature in 1838 authorized
a loan of $4,000,000 for enlargements.

The plan was to borrow as long as the surplus tolls
afforded means of paying the interest, and to make no provision whatever for paying the principal. The result was to
destroy the confidence of money-lenders to such a degree
"that in the fall of 1841 and the winter of 1842 the 6 per
cent stock of the state, which in 1833 bore 20 per cent premium, were not salable at 20 per cent discount, and great
lots were sold at a depreciation of twenty-two cents on each
dollar of stock."

When the legislature assembled in January,
1842, it became evident that over $1,000,000 was
due the contractors, and that the state was on the
verge of bankruptcy. The assembly was forced to
pass drastic measures to relieve the tension. The
"stop and tax law of 1842" was immediately enacted, and "all expenditures for construction were
suspended, and only necessary expenditures for
maintenance and repairs were allowed."[1]

One desirable effect of the panic upon the citizens of New York State, however, was the increased interest in agricultural pursuits. Men began
to realize, as a result of the commercial revulsion,
that by labor alone could wealth be acquired. Fairs
and cattle shows throughout the state were attended

[1] Sowers, *Financial History of New York*, pp. 68–70.

by increasing multitudes, not of farmers alone, but of all groups of society. The exhibit of agricultural products, of animals, articles of domestic manufacture, and farming implements at the state fair at Rochester, in 1844, was highly creditable to the citizens of the state. With a few exceptions, by that date all the counties in the state had organized agricultural societies, and were making useful advances "in collecting practical or various matters connected with the tillage of the soil, economy in the application of labor, improvements in farming implements, and in the breed of animals." Agricultural as well as mechanical labor by 1845 was taking its just and honorable position in the estimation of all classes, as against the speculative endeavors that had plunged the state into the distress of the thirties.[1]

In the meantime, how fared the other eastern states? The governor of New Hampshire congratulated his fellow-citizens in June, 1837, on the sound condition of the state's finances, which he attributed to the fact that the state government had not indulged in extravagant internal improvement schemes. "Our improvements by canals and railroads have been left exclusively to private enterprise," announced the executive, and he recommended that the state "pledge the public faith to no

---

[1] *New York Senate Journal* (1843), p. 5; *ibid.* (1844), p. 24; *ibid.* (1845), p. 37.

expenditures for these objects." By 1838 New Hampshire could boast that it was burdened with no permanent debt; that it owed little or nothing; while in contracts to many other states, it had a fund of $25,000 in the stock of the New Hampshire bank, from which it derived an annual income. Beyond passing acts to relieve debtors in 1837, regulating circulation so as not to exceed the capital stock actually paid in, providing for the redemption of notes of small denominations, and for individual liability to apply to all banks and corporations, New Hampshire was not compelled to enact stringent banking laws. The greatest hardship in New Hampshire came through the circulation of fractional coins within the state from beyond its limits. It became a matter of "speculation and profit to collect and send specie out of the state, and to bring in to supply in its place the depreciated bills of other states." Aside from this inconvenience, the citizens of New Hampshire had much less to complain of than many of their neighbors. As was stated, in 1842 they had much reason to rejoice that so much prosperity and success had attended their efforts. This does not mean that they escaped entirely the hardships of these years. But it is true that they did not feel the burdens as excessive as those of some of their neighboring states. This was undoubtedly due to the pursuits of the people of New Hampshire, to their conservatism in embarking on foolish internal improvement policies, and to the conduct of their banks in assisting the public. As the committee on banking reported in 1841, "the bank bills in circulation do not appear to be redundant when compared with the probable wants and convenience of the community, nor to be in such abundance as to exceed proper and safe limits, as they relate to the means provided for their redemption."[1]

In similar manner Vermont could report that her citizens had suffered perhaps less than those of other states, although she acknowledged in 1837 that the business and credit systems had received a serious shock. Her citizens could not point, however, to the public interest of her speedy recovery. An examination of the affairs of the Bank of Bennington disclosed questionable practices upon the part of one of its directors, while certain of the banks increased their circulation after suspension of specie payment as others contracted. For example, the Bank of Manchester had in May, 1837, less than $70,000 in circulation; but on January 9, 1838, the amount of bills in circulation was over $140,000, revealing an increase of $70,000 in eight months. There was some alleviation of the pressure by the resumption of 1838, but the panic of 1839 continued

---

[1] *New Hampshire Senate Journal* (1837), p. 15; *ibid.* (1838), pp. 17, 18, 23; *ibid.* (1840), pp. 12, 13; *ibid.* (1841), p. 368; *New Hampshire Statutes* (1837), p. 308; (1838), pp. 337, 343, 344, 388; (1840), p. 469; (1841), p. 539.

to make conditions extremely hard in Vermont throughout 1840.[1]

The same evils and reactions were recorded in Connecticut, New Jersey, and Delaware. None of these states had debts; and although the laboring classes, particularly in Newark, New Jersey, complained of hardships, the state government passed through the crisis unscathed. Connecticut experienced difficulty, owing to the abuses of certain of its banks; and the New Jersey banks, located as they were, between New York and Philadelphia, were more or less affected by the financial operations of these cities. All these states reported the greatest pressure in the mercantile districts, and all passed rigid banking laws to curb the abuses revealed by the stringency.[2]

The vicissitudes of Pennsylvania during these years are of absorbing interest. Biddle endeavored to maintain his institution at the time of the general collapse by inducing the other banks to unite in upholding the United States Bank. When they refused, he, along with others, suspended;[3] and then he began his cotton manipulations and obstruction policy regarding resumption, that will be explained

[1] *Vermont House Journal* (1837), p. 14; *Senate Journal* (1838), p. 9; *Senate Journal* (1840), App., pp. 27, 28.

[2] For Connecticut, cf. *Exec. Doc., Twenty-fifth Cong., Second Sess.*, Doc. 79, pp. 177, 178, 190–98; *New Jersey Assembly* (1837), pp. 146–49; (1843), pp. 16, 17; *Delaware Senate Journal* (1841), p. 5.

[3] Galpin to Van Buren, May 11, 1837, Van Buren MSS.

in another chapter. At the close of the year the governor declared Pennsylvania had weathered the storm remarkably well. This, he explained, was owing to the general prosperity of the preceding years, which had left business in good condition to bear the strain; to the fact that the debts, to the banks particularly, were either diminished, or generally of a temporary kind incurred for mere present accommodation; to the successful completion of a portion of the public works, which provided means of transportation for the products of remote districts to nearby markets; to the law prohibiting the circulation of small notes, which had restrained the increase of paper circulation and had increased the proportion of specie in the hands of the community and the banks; to the stabilizing influence of the United States Bank; and to the character of the mercantile business of Philadelphia, whose debtors, generally residing in the agricultural regions of the West, were not so materially affected by the derangement of trade as those depending on the southern cotton, tobacco, and sugar plantations. "Her claims on other states have been," continued the writer, "generally secured, and the effect of her credit, and that of her institutions, have been salutary in proportion." The report of the auditor-general showed by the close of 1837 a decrease of one-fourth in amount of bank-note circulation since suspension, of one-fifth of their discounts, of one-twentieth of their deposits, and an increase of one-half in their specie. Moreover, the prices of land and of produce, and all other articles had neither decreased nor experienced a sudden rise which betokened a want of confidence in the soundness of the currency.[1]

But Pennsylvania, like other states, could not keep out spurious paper notes. These were issued, without authority of law, by individuals and corporations, and were forced into circulation to supply the place of specie which was either locked up by the banks awaiting resumption, or hoarded by its possessors. When resumption did take place the next year, business revived, only to collapse entirely with the crash of the United States Bank in 1839. Then, in truth, Pennsylvania began to experience the full fruits of her follies.[2]

The effects of these two crises fell with greatest force on the mercantile community. As the governor said in 1840, there was a more essential difference between the position of the citizens of the state

in a pecuniary point of view in that year than in the years 1816–18. Then a spirit of speculation had infected the agricultural as well as all other portions of the community. Now, however, our farmers are generally out of debt and in flourishing circumstances, and it is the mercantile and manufacturing classes that have been principally suffering from

[1] *Pennsylvania House Journal*, II (1837), 10–16.

[2] *Pennsylvania Senate Journal*, I (1838), 175, 183.

the undue expansion of the credit system. But there was now an evil of which we then knew nothing, and which does more than counterbalance the partial exemption from the suffering of our agricultural interest.[1]

This was the contraction of enormous foreign debts by the states to carry on their internal improvements. By 1842, Pennsylvania was forced to abandon her projects at a time when her affairs were in complete chaos, and her laboring classes, who had suffered grievously for five years, were in their worst condition.[2]

The period of the panic also marked important changes in the manufacturing industries of the East. In the making of boots and shoes, the transition from the merchant employer to the factory owner was hastened by the failure of many of the older firms. "Financial embarrassments impressed on Chauncey Jerome the need of wider markets for clocks, and led to the introduction of brass works and the beginning of foreign trade in that article." This stimulated the entire metal-working industry, while Manila paper made from old rope, and changes in fabrics were brought about by the emergencies of the day. The manufacture of fancy cassimeres, carpets, ingrain rugs, and domett flannels testified to the technical improvements in woolens, and the steady progress in this industry. But these beneficial results were more than over-

---

[1] *Ibid.*, I (1840), 24, 25.   [2] *Op. cit.*, I (1841), 14.

shadowed by the hardships endured by the states and the citizens of the East during these years of travail.[1]

Turning to the South, we find the conditions even worse in certain localities than in the East. By the fall of 1836 the southern states began to evince signs of distress, and when the crash actually took place, the blow fell with heaviest force upon the Cotton Belt. The Old South did not escape from under the blow, but in comparison with the havoc wrought in Mississippi, Alabama, and Louisiana, the citizens of the Old South had much for which to be grateful.

Maryland seems to have suffered more than Virginia or North and South Carolina. Baltimore experienced the same hardships as other commercial centers, while the extensive internal improvement plans were a heavy drain upon the state's finances. When the canal commissioners went abroad in 1837 to sell the eight millions of dollars of state bonds to carry out the proposed scheme, they found it impossible to dispose of them at the stipulated price. On their return they concluded an agreement with the Chesapeake and Ohio Canal Company and the Baltimore and Ohio Railroad Company for the sale of a large portion of the bonds, amounting to $6,000,000. At the December session of the legislature in 1837, the assembly refused to ratify this

[1] Clark, *History of Manufactures*, pp. 380, 381.

agreement "because it was apprehended that the companies might be compelled to sacrifice the credit of the state"; but they consented to a modification of the plan, "which required that none of the bonds should be transferred from the possession of the commissioner of loans till their equivalent in money was paid into the treasury." At the same session, however, the legislature ordered the delivery of stock to the Chesapeake and Ohio Canal Company to the amount of $2,500,000. The bonds thus delivered were transferred "to banks and capitalists on both sides of the Atlantic, to be held as pledges for temporary loans, or sold, at the option of the holders, for whatever discredited stock would bring in a depressed market." By 1842 the company was in debt over $1,000,000, and as the legislature refused to render further aid, work on the canal came to a standstill. By that year the Baltimore and Ohio Railroad had reached Cumberland, and "the state-secured script was down to fifty cents on the dollar."[1]

The citizens of Virginia and North and South Carolina did not escape, however, the direful effects of the panic. The inability of the planters to dispose of their crops, together with the financial difficulties of the banks, compelled the Virginians to demand

[1] *Maryland Senate Journal* (1837), pp. 9, 10; (1842), pp. 7, 8; *Annual Report of Baltimore and Ohio* (1837), p. 4; *Report of Chesapeake and Ohio* (1851), pp. 77, 78; Meyer, *History of Transportation*, p. 405.

stay laws, and abandon their internal improvement project. The resumption in 1838 was followed by the stringency of 1839 and more insistent demands for relief from the legislature during the forties.[1] South Carolina suffered a want of small coin for the ordinary purposes of life.[2] North Carolina reported a depreciation of 50 per cent on most tangible and active property, on land yet more, lots scarcely selling for the cost of improvement, and farms yielding about 2 per cent of their value.[3]

The most significant outcome of the crisis in these states was the increased interest in diversifying the crops. This, as well as the general condition of the South, was clearly brought out in the message of the governor of South Carolina in 1840:

Amid the general pressure of the times we have suffered but little, while thousands and tens of thousands of our fellow citizens in other sections of the country have been overwhelmed in poverty and ruin. Go from neighborhood to neighborhood throughout our territory, and, with the most inconsiderable exceptions, everywhere you meet the evidences of comfort and plenty. . . . . The spirit of emigration to the fertile valleys of the West, which drove so many of our people from their native soil, has in a great measure subsided, and been succeeded by a patriotic devotion which every succeeding year serves to strengthen. The lessons of

[1] *Virginia House Journal* (1837), pp. 4, 5; (1839), p. 1; (1841–42), Doc. 71.

[2] *Reports and Resolutions, South Carolina* (1837), p. 2.

[3] *North Carolina Senate and House Journals* (1840–41), pp. 335, 336.

dearly bought experience have not been without profit. . . . .
It is a matter of sincere pride that our leading interest, agriculture, is now attracting unusual attention. . . . . Many of
our planters begin almost to doubt the sanity of that man
who will make his cotton, and buy everything else. Many
dissent from the hitherto received maxim in our agricultural
philosophy, that the most successful planter is he who sends
the largest number of bales to his factory. The modest and
unpretending farmer, who makes everything that he wants,
and by a sure and regular surplus adds steadily to his property, has forced himself upon public attention, and contributed largely to dissipate general and mischievous error.
. . . . The strongest desire now pervades our community
to develop to the utmost the agricultural and other natural
resources of the state.[1]

Edmund Ruffin was employed by the legislature to make an agricultural survey of the state,
with the idea of recommending improvements; and
his work was ably seconded by the newspapers and
agricultural journals, and the efforts of ex-Governor
J. H. Hammond, of South Carolina, Jethro V.
Jones, of Georgia, Dr. N. B. Cloud, of Alabama,
and Dr. Martin W. Philips, of Mississippi.[2]
Throughout the whole Southland there was a movement for reform which was augmented by the distress of these years.

But it was in the lower South where the real
pressure was felt. As early as the fall of 1836, land
speculators in Mississippi writing to their promot-

[1] *South Carolina House and Senate Journals* (1840), pp. 10, 11.

[2] Phillips, *American Negro Slavery*, p. 215.

ers in the East began to complain of the money stringency. The prospects that the price of cotton would fall still lower kept merchants from buying. In Alabama, property almost entirely changed hands; in Mobile, by May, 1837, there was not a solvent house; and Biddle was besought by the mayor and aldermen of the city for financial aid early in the crisis.[1] Money which heretofore had been treated as if "any man might make it with a wish" was now extremely scarce. The cause for this was the fact that heretofore the credit of the South had been altogether overrated, and now it was unduly underrated. The region still had great resources, but the people, unable to meet their debts, were hard pressed by their creditors, with the result that the market steadily declined. Negroes formerly worth $1,200 to $1,500 each could be bought in Mississippi for $250 to $200 cash.[2] The loss on this property alone was enough to bankrupt the state. But the misfortune did not stop there.

Many of the planters of Mississippi had anticipated their crops, and had received and expended three-fourths of their value months in advance. The consequence was the complete bankruptcy of many planters. In their dilemma those whose crops had been from one hundred to seven hundred bales found themselves forced to sacrifice many of their slaves in

[1] Poe to Biddle, September 6, 1836, B.P.

[2] *National Intelligencer*, May 3, 1837.

order to get the common necessaries of life for the support of themselves and the rest of their negroes.

In one instance a small planter, whose hopes ran high in 1836, and who owned twenty-two slaves, sold three of his best men in 1837, for whom he actually paid $3,200, for $850, to buy pork and corn for the remainder.[1]

The currency of the state was in a terrible condition, as the banks refused to pay coin, and proposed to shave their paper. By 1839 extensive plantations were thrown out of cultivation and lying waste for want of hands to till them, the slaves having been seized under execution and carried off by the sheriff. The greatest embarrassments in Mississippi were mostly confined to the old counties, as the new counties had been created and settled too late to embark in the extravagant purchases of land and negroes at twice their value which had been so common within recent years in the lower counties. Northern Mississippi was in debt for land bought at fair prices, of which generally one-third was paid. But what impressed travelers in the state during these years was the attempt of planters to free themselves from the dependence upon a single crop. One such visitor declares he saw corn and wheat fields, hogs, and cattle, about the plantations, and in many instances the planters' daughters at the spinning wheel and loom, and their sons at the plow.[2]

[1] *Cincinnati Daily Gazette*, May 8, 1837.

[2] Bolton to Curtis, May 18, 1839, New York and Mississippi Land Co. MSS.

A North Carolinian traveling through the state in 1840 did not hesitate to say that the hard times of Mississippi exceeded those in all other sections.

Lands . . . . that once commanded from twenty to fifty dollars per acre may now be bought for three or five dollars, and that with considerable improvements, while many have been sold at sheriff sales at 50 cents, that were considered worth ten to twenty dollars. The people, too, were running their negroes to Texas and to Alabama, and leaving their real estate and perishable property to be sold, or rather sacrificed. . . . . So great is the panic, and so dreadful the distress, that there are a great many farms prepared to receive crops, and some of them actually planted, and yet deserted, not a human being to be found upon them.[1]

Every newspaper that came from Mississippi was filled with advertisements of negroes and lands to be sold in satisfaction of judgments. The whole community was prostrated; and finally, in 1842, the state was driven to repudiate its obligations.

New Orleans, like New York, was stricken by a general depression in business. Within three days after Jackson retired, the failures in New Orleans took place, "after which they succeeded each other with fearful rapidity." Beginning with March, the reports from New Orleans grew more discouraging day by day. The operations in cotton or other products soon were limited to small sales, and everything was involved in mist and secrecy in the city. By April 13 the citizens of New Orleans petitioned

[1] Wills, diary quoted in Phillips, *op. cit.*, pp. 372, 373.

for a relief law. Niles, for April 15, declared the southern merchants could not pay five cents on the dollar of what they owed to New York. By the nineteenth, cotton was a drug on the market, selling from 11 to 15 cents. On the twenty-first the *National Intelligencer* declared, "not a bale of cotton, not a hogshead of tobacco, was shipped yesterday from this port." The close of the year saw a slight revival in the trade, although none could claim that business, in any of its branches, had yet grown very brisk. Business remained curtailed throughout the following year, and by July of 1839 the *New Orleans Courier* announced that times were now harder, "according to common report, than they were during the embargo, or the war with England."[1] In the same year the banks of Louisiana suspended a second time:

Not because they had suffered losses which compelled them to it, but only because they feared to be drained of their specie in consequence of the suspension of which the Pennsylvania banks had set the example. This measure met with the general approbation of the public, who thought they saw in this cessation of action on the part of the moneyed institutions the means of preserving their strength, and of keeping them ready to resume their legal direction and duties as soon as the resumption of the other banks would permit it without danger.

For two years they remained suspended, during which time their available means diminished $300,-

[1] Quoted in *Cincinnati Daily Gazette*, August 6, 1839.

ooo, while their liabilities increased more than $780,000; and when the legislature was about to convene in 1841, the banks decided to continue this state of affairs until November, 1842, on the ground that they were unable to provide the funds "to meet the payment of such of their cash liability as [might] be immediately demanded of them, while their circulation [was] only sustained by the confidence inspired by its being received at the other banks." Public opinion, however, forced the banks to attempt resumption, which some very reluctantly entered upon. In May, 1842, the banks of New Orleans resumed specie payment, only to be forced to suspend after an operation of sixteen days, a situation produced, according to *Hunt's Merchants' Magazine*, by the bickerings between the banks themselves. Whatever might be the cause, the money market in New Orleans and throughout the state remained in a doleful condition throughout the years 1842 and 1843.[1]

Georgia and Florida also felt the ravages of the money stringency though perhaps not to the extent of Louisiana, Alabama, and Mississippi. There was sufficient coin in circulation in Georgia in 1837 to carry on ordinary exchanges, and the debtor class was relieved from the severity of the times "by the magnanimous forbearance of many of their credit-

[1] *Hunt's Merchants' Magazine*, VII, 77, 78; *Louisiana House Journal* (1841–42), p. 3.

ors, and the timely aid afforded by the Central Bank." Florida and Georgia did not feel the full effects of their follies until the forties. The citizens of Florida boasted of their tranquillity and the punctuality of their payments until 1839; but by 1840 the per capita debt of the territory was near $200, and the next year she had to acknowledge that specie had disappeared; her court dockets thronged with suits, and the necessaries, to say nothing of the luxuries of life, vending at enormous prices. Every portion of the territory was suffering, the middle district more than others. Finally, in 1841, Florida was compelled to repudiate her debts.[1]

A flood of banking legislation was enacted by the southern legislatures to remedy many of the abuses of the preceding years. These laws generally called for the appointment of bank commissioners by the governor of the state, with power to investigate the books of the institution, limitations on circulation, investments, and liabilities; penalties for failure to pay in specie; restrictions on officers, directors, or stockholders becoming indebted to the bank, or borrowing from it on the pledge of their stock. In Virginia the directors were restrained from discounting or purchasing notes rejected by the bank;

[1] *Georgia Senate Journal* (1837), p. 10; (1838), p. 21; (1840), p. 9; (1842), pp. 16, 17; *Florida Senate Journal* (1839), p. 7; (1840), p. 111; (1841), pp. 11, 12.

in Alabama annual statements were required of the liabilities of the president and directors, and their securities; also the indebtedness of each and every member of the general assembly, with their securities; while in Georgia it was specifically provided that "no stockholder or any officer shall borrow money from the pledge of his stock, but shall give the same security as other borrowers, and such security shall not be another director or stockholder." Mississippi prohibited its banks from dealing in cotton as security or collateral for a loan, or purchasing "as an article of trade, any cotton or other commodity"; while Florida made the officers of the bank that suspended specie payment for sixty days liable to punishment as felons with imprisonment for five years or a fine of $20,000.[1]

Thus the South paid dearly in the years following the panic for its former misdeeds. The Old South did not feel the hardships to the extent of the lower South, but each district, as well as each state, experienced difficulties in proportion to its previous rashness. The lower South was most grievously affected, owing to its laxness in banking procedure, its reliance upon a single crop, and its wild internal improvement projects. But throughout the whole area an increased interest in diversifying the crops,

---

[1] *Virginia Statutes* (1840), pp. 53–55; *Alabama Statutes* (1839), p. 64; *Georgia Statutes* (1838), pp. 31–43; *Mississippi Statutes* (1840), pp. 13–21; *Florida Statutes* (1843), pp. 57, 58.

and an attempt to make the South more self-sufficient was stimulated by the distress.

Contrary to the generally accepted opinion, the pressure in the West in no way compared to that of the East and South until after the collapse of 1839; then it more than equaled the distress of other sections. The embarrassment in the West was not felt to any great degree in Illinois in the middle of June, 1837, whereas the stringency in other areas began in March.[1] The reason for this may be found in the respective pursuits of the several districts. Ohio, Indiana, and Illinois were agricultural rather than manufacturing or commercial states, and therefore they had not participated to the same degree in overtrading as the East and South. Furthermore, the good crops of 1837 came to the relief of the farmers.[2] As the *Maysville Eagle* for April 29, 1837, said:

The West has not felt, and will not feel the money pressure as severely as the North and South. It is true, our great staples—flour, pork, hemp, and tobacco—are down and coming down, but generally, the farmers and merchants are prudent, and have not overtraded to the same extent which has occurred in the North and South. We have not heard of a

[1] *Illinois Senate Journal* (1837), p. 16.

[2] On the crop situation there is an abundance of material in the western papers. Cf. *Cin. Daily Gazette*, June 23, July 18, 1837, for citations from many western papers. For general conditions of Indiana and Illinois in 1837, and their fairly prosperous condition, cf. *N.Y. Journal of Commerce*, November 25, 1837.

single failure in Kentucky of any magnitude since the commencement of the pressure.[1]

Four months later the *New York Journal of Commerce*, quoting a western account, reiterated and reaffirmed the belief, in the following manner:

> The pressure of the times begins to be pretty hard in this country, though we hope and believe it will not be here what it has been and is at the East. Considering the recent settlement of the country, business and improvements are going on in a lively way. . . . . Farming is flourishing and there is an exceedingly fine prospect at this time of the most beautiful crops for the present year.[2]

The *Cincinnati Chronicle* commented on the brisk building-program and crowded aspects of Cincinnati, though acknowledging that the derangement of the currency had injured the manufactures, commerce, and local improvements of the city.[3] The governor of Ohio substantiated these statements in his annual message of 1839, announcing that the pressure under which the citizens were laboring had not fallen with the same force on Ohio as on some other portions of the Union. "This," wrote the executive, "is owing to the fact that we are more an agricultural, than a manufacturing or commercial, people; and, comparatively speaking, but little in debt. . . . . The

---

[1] *Maysville Eagle*, April 29, 1837.

[2] *New York Journal of Commerce*, August 11, 1837.

[3] *Cin. Chronicle*, quoted in *Cin. Daily Gazette*, July 3, 1837.

mechanical and agricultural portion of the community, being generally out of debt, have not experienced the same embarrassments that have been felt by the merchants, and those engaged in heavy business demanding large capital and extensive credit."[1] The deposit bank in Cincinnati assured the secretary of the treasury of the "sound condition of our community."[2] The committee investigating the banks agreed that the great mass of the farmers were wealthy, but as all the farmers, mechanics, and every class of society were in debt, and perhaps mostly to the merchants, the pressure of the merchants on their debtors would inevitably affect the former's status. As the committee said, the people were debtors to the banks, and not the banks to the people, as many supposed.[3] From Indiana the report came of no failures of consequence among the business men in 1837. The suits for debt in the courts were not more numerous than usual. Sheriff sales seldom occurred. All the produce of the country was demanded for consumption, and emigration to the state was increasing.[4] The Committee on Public Works in Illinois in June, 1837, said the embarrassment of the eastern and southern states

[1] *Ohio Doc., Thirty-eighth General Assembly*, Doc. 1, p. 7.

[2] *Senate Doc., Twenty-fifth Cong., Second Sess.*, Vol. IV, Doc. 365, No. 54.

[3] *Op. cit.*, Vol. VI, Doc. 471, pp. 447, 448.

[4] *Indiana Senate Journal* (1837), p. 64.

had not yet visited the state. "The limited banking capital of our state," declared the Committee, "has prevented an accumulation of indebtedness. The value of our lands has heretofore induced large investments of eastern capital, which has generally resulted for the benefit of our citizens, and there has been, comparatively, but little overtrading in our commercial community; consequently that despondency which is hanging over other states is not seriously felt in this."[1] The governors of Indiana and Kentucky thanked Providence for the profusion of their crops, and their own favorable situation at the close of 1837.[2]

By 1839 the aspect of affairs in the West had changed. A general fall in agricultural prices was noted, which was rendered inevitable from two causes: the abundance of the present year's products, and the scarcity of money. As the *National Intelligencer* said, the pressure that for two years had been weighing so heavily upon merchants and manufacturers was now, for the first time, reaching the agriculturist.

In 1837 and 1838 the country presented the anomaly of high prices of the products of the soil at the same time that there existed a distressing scarcity of money. It was a severe time upon the consumers, but a golden harvest to producers.

---

[1] *Illinois Senate Journal* (1837), p. 16.

[2] *Kentucky Senate Journal* (1837), p. 21; *Indiana Senate Journal* (1837), p. 8. On general conditions of Ohio and Indiana, cf. Pooley, *Settlement of Illinois*, p. 347.

Now, however, the scale has turned the other way; and although the people of the city are still crushed under the all-pervading pressure of the money market, they are relieved from the exorbitant exactions imposed upon them by monopolists of the first necessities of life. The farmers are the last to experience the evil, and it is fair to infer that they will be the last to find relief.[1]

With agricultural productiveness exceeding demand by 1839, and an insufficient amount of money to answer as a medium of exchange, western indebtedness to eastern merchants had to be liquidated in produce, at reduced prices, or in money, at a time of universal contraction in the currency.[2] Then, in truth, the West began to reap the harvest it had sown in the early years of the decade. The interest on money ranged from 10 to 50 per cent. Counterfeit and bogus coin circulated in this district. Barter was resorted to in Illinois to carry on trade, and "notes were sometimes drawn, payable in a cow, or a horse, or other farm products."[3] By 1841, one-third of the banking institutions of Ohio had failed, and the people's wrath toward the banks broke out in riots.[4] Wisconsin and Michigan were inundated with spurious paper currency, while from

[1] *Pittsburg Daily Advocate*, quoted in *National Intelligencer*, August 17, 1839.

[2] *Ohio Doc., Thirty-ninth General Assembly*, Doc. 21, pp. 5, 6.

[3] Pooley, *op. cit.*, p. 569.

[4] *Ohio Senate Journal* (1842), pp. 13, 14; McMaster, *History of the People of the United States*, VII, 6, 7.

Tennessee, Kentucky, and Arkansas like reports came of the depreciation of property and the want of a circulating medium.

Needless to say, the internal improvement plans of the western states were suspended with the terrible distress of the forties. It will be recalled that Illinois, in 1836, had projected six railroads and as many new canals, and had provided for the improvement of the Kaskaskia, Illinois, Great and Little Wabash, and Rock rivers. Furthermore, it had been ordered that work on all these roads should commence simultaneously. The result was that many of these enterprises were begun, but none was completed. "When the labor ceased, no one improvement was finished in any one particular. A single railroad might be in all degrees of completeness, while in many places the work had not even been started."[1] This crisis was precipitated by the close connection between the Illinois banks and the internal improvement schemes. Many of the banks were fiscal agents for the canals and the railroads, and "if they went down, they would carry the canal and internal improvement schemes in their train."[2] A special session of the legislature was quickly summoned, which legalized the suspension of specie payment by the banks, but

[1] "Governor's Letter Books," in *Illinois Historical Collections*, II, 52.

[2] Ford, *History of Illinois*, pp. 191, 192.

refused to touch the subject of internal improvements. "As a last resort, many of the canal contractors made a proposition to take canal script and bonds from the state in lieu of money, preferring to do this rather than suffer on account of a cessation of labor on the canals." This afforded only temporary relief. "Many of the late purchasers of bonds failed to make payments as agreed upon, and the credit of the state declined still further."[1] Finally, in 1838, the board of commissioners determined to suspend operations under all new contracts, and to curtail their expenditures within the narrowest possible limits.[2] In October of 1839, John Wright and Company of London, which had taken about one million dollars' worth of the first bonds issued in 1837, failed. This embarrassed to a still greater degree the credit of the state. By this time the sentiment of the people of Illinois had changed toward the subject of internal improvements, and in December, 1839, a resolution was passed to instruct the Committee on Internal Improvements "to inquire into the expediency of suspending all further operations on the various railroads in the state."[3] "Thus terminated," explained the governor in his message of 1842, "our unfortunate and short-lived scheme of internal improvements, leav-

[1] *Illinois Historical Collections*, VII, 66.
[2] *Report of Board of Public Works in Illinois* (1843), p. 4.
[3] *Illinois Senate Journal* (1839), p. 33.

ing the state with less than thirty miles of a single railroad completed, out of a multitude projected, with an immense debt overwhelming her, and without any permanent means whatever provided to meet the interest that was so rapidly accruing upon it."[1]

Other states which had entered recklessly upon these plans endured the same difficulties. In 1837 Ohio had projected six great canal works, and had pledged herself to give one-third of the authorized capital. This extended system of internal improvements involved a great expenditure with very little prospect of immediate returns, and yet the people continued to spend large sums on these works. By 1839 the state appropriations for canals had reached the enormous sum of $366,000. All work was now suspended, and for the next five years a rigid policy of retrenchment was carried out.[2] Kentucky, Indiana, Tennessee, and Michigan experienced the same difficulties.

The poor man and the laborer, as usual, bore the brunt of the catastrophe. In New York City alone, in 1837, it was said that "six thousand masons and carpenters and other workmen connected with building had been discharged." Niles records that by September, 1837, nine-tenths of the

---

[1] *Illinois Senate Journal* (1842–43), p. 12.

[2] Morris, "Internal Improvements in Ohio," in *Amer. Hist. Assoc. Papers*, III, 128; *Hunt's Merchants' Magazine*, XXI, 405; Bogart, *Financial History of Ohio*, pp. 80, 307–309.

factories in the eastern states had closed, and that the same proportion of employees had been discharged. From Dover, Massachusetts, came word that a mill there closed its doors throwing "two hundred females and forty males" out of work. "The streets of Bedford," said one report, "are now thronged with seamen out of employment. Forty whale ships are lying at the wharves, but nothing doing to fit them out for sea." Haverford, Massachusetts, announced "the almost entire failure of the shoe business in this vicinity"; while similar accounts came from the manufacturers of Lynn and Salem. Many of the dry-goods jobbing houses of New York were in a state of bankruptcy by the close of 1837 on account of the stringency on the South. Trade unions found themselves nullified at a blow. The competitors for work were so numerous that strikes were far from being the order of the day. The hardships among the laboring classes were intense. One-half to two-thirds of the clerks and salesmen in large commercial houses in Philadelphia were without work by June, 1837.[1] Mothers were begging in the streets of New York for their children by the close of the year. The almshouses and poorhouses were full to the brim, while hundreds unable to gain admittance suffered from cold and starvation. As the cold months came on

[1] Niles, April 22, September 16, 1837; *Nat. Intell.*, April 18, 1837; Commons, *History of Labor*, I, 455.

"the suffering of the poor became so aggravated, and the number of unemployed increased to such a degree, that the ordinary means were inadequate to relieve even those who were destitute of every one of the necessities of life. Some died of starvation. Some were frozen to death. Many, through exposure and privation, contracted fatal diseases. A large number who had never before known want were reduced to beg. Respectable mechanics were known to offer their services as waiters in eating-houses for their food." Advertisements for help brought forth overwhelming responses from all grades of society, showing that people were only too willing to work if they could secure it. The winter of 1838 was unusually severe, thereby aggravating the suffering of the poor, while the number of unemployed increased daily. The spring brought a little relief, but the hard times of 1839 again threw many out of employment. The condition of the laborer steadily declined, reaching its lowest point in 1841.[1]

The professional and salaried classes weathered the storm for a while better than any other group. As the *New York Journal of Commerce* says:

The calamity attaches to the whole community, with a few exceptions, such as lawyers, notaries, and salaried men.

[1] *A Brief Popular Account of the Financial Panics in United States to 1857,* by members of the New York Press, p. 30. (Pamphlet.)

These last, who a year ago considered their condition unfortunate, inasmuch as their salaries were not (in general) advanced with the increased price of rents and provisions, now begin to feel comfortable. As a class, they were so poor and in such feeble credit, when the artificial advancement of property came on, that they were unable to embark in the adventures of the day, even had they been so disposed; and the result is that the storm passes harmlessly over their heads while it sweeps down others who but recently were considered beyond the contingencies of accidents.[1]

But with the general collapse of the banks and all forms of industrial enterprise, together with the increased cost of living and the cutting of wages, their lot became as strenuous, if not more so, than their fellow-workers.

It was upon the well-to-do land operators in the West and the eastern capitalist who had invested so heavily in lands that the panic fell with the greatest force. These men who had risked so much during the years of inflation were now groaning under the heavy load they had to carry. The private correspondence of Solomon Juneau, one of the co-founders of Milwaukee, and of Moses M. Strong, a land agent for wealthy eastern speculators, clearly disclosed the state of mind of this class of eastern capitalists. Juneau pressed his friend and debtor, Martin, for funds, for, as he said, times were awful in Milwaukee; while Strong was cautioned by his

[1] *New York Journal of Commerce*, May 9, 1837.

employers to manage his land purchases in a prudent manner.[1]

In the midst of the distress, the *New York Journal of Commerce* advanced this sagacious advice to employers:

We see that some of the trades societies are holding meetings to reduce wages. There is more wisdom in this than usually governs the proceedings of such bodies. We presume, however, that wages would come down without being voted down, so that the labor of voting was quite lost. By the way, we hope the employers will to the full adopt the English policy, and employ no men who do not forever abjure the unions. The good of the laborers and the peace of society demand this course. Now is the time to deliver mechanics and their families from the cruel oppression of the unions. It should be done thoroughly. The rules of the unions as to hours, pay, and everything else ought to be thoroughly broken up. The ten-hour system is one of the worst deformities of their deformed code. To work only ten hours in summer and eight hours in winter is to waste life. No man can prosper who does not abandon such rules.[2]

Such statements as these, together with conventions of business men calling upon their associates to elect only representatives favorable to their interests,[3] along with the bank suspensions, which

[1] Martin MSS, September 20, October 7, 1836; July 14, September 9, October 20, December 1, 1837; Strong MSS, July 28, 1837; January 29, 1841; July 14, 1842.

[2] *N.Y. Journal of Commerce*, quoted in *Cin. Daily Gazette*, May 23, 1837.

[3] Cf. account of business men's convention in Philadelphia, in *Cin. Daily Gazette*, November 24, 1837.

the state legislatures legalized, were the sparks which lighted the flames of the workingmen's discontent. As the duplicity of the banks became more and more evident, the hatred for all such institutions and for the whole credit system grew apace. As Eli Moore, a Tammany representative of the labor element of New York City, expressed it on the floor of Congress:

The people [whom he identified with the laboring classes] are neither so unwise or so unreasonable as either to expect or desire a perfect equality of wealth. . . . . The people, the democracy, contend for no measure that does not hold out to individual enterprise proper motives for exertion. All they ask is that the great principle upon which the government is founded, the principle of equal rights, should be faithfully observed and carried out, to the exclusion of all exclusive privileges.[1]

In such an atmosphere was conceived the Equal Rights party, the riots, the lynching, and mob violence of this decade. As the committee on banking and corporations in the Illinois Legislature said in 1843:

Our revolutionary fathers abolished the laws of entail and primogeniture, and thereby imagined they had placed an insuperable barrier against concentration of property. We, however, have devised means through the agency of corporations of concentrating the largest amount of property and wealth, and of holding and transmitting it in perpetuity. They abolished hereditary ranks and made provision against titled nobility. We have created the nobles without a title;

[1] Quoted in Trimble, *op. cit.*, p. 396.

we omit the shadow but retain the substance; we have not only the most numerous, but also the most powerful body of nobles that now exist, or ever existed, in any country on earth, endowed by law with privileges greater than were ever before conferred on any body of men. What aristocratic privilege was ever equal to that of controlling the currency of seventeen millions of people, and making money plenty [plentiful] or scarce at pleasure? What privilege could be compared to that of controlling the value of all property in the nation, and raising or falling [lowering] prices at pleasure, of controlling the credit of every man in the nation, and raising or depressing it at pleasure? What privilege could be compared to that of making money out of nothing, and almost without limit, and loaning it at usurious rates of interest? Such are some of the privileges conferred on our banks by law; compared to which the feudal privileges of the barons of other days and other lands were insignificant baubles.[1]

It is not strange, in the light of these statements, that men like Biddle were alarmed by the Jack Cade utterances of labor; that Van Buren's apparent acquiescence in the Locofoco doctrines caused consternation; that rigorous corporation laws were enacted following the crisis; or that the teachings of Robert Owen and Albert Brisbane aroused intense interest in this country.[2]

There was, however, some justification for this popular hatred of banks, as an account of the "fiscal rascality and depredation on the public in

[1] *Illinois Senate and House Reports*, II (1842), 191–93.

[2] On Owen and Brisbane, cf. Hayes, *Social Politics in the United States*, chap. ii.

one year, as published in the newspapers from time to time," disclosed. According to this list, the practices shown (Table I) were placed at the doors of the banking officials.

TABLE I

Whole capital of the United States Bank	$35,000,000
Schuylkill Bank, robbed by cashier	1,300,000
Manhattan Bank, robbed by Newton	50,000
Virginia Bank, robbed by Dabney	500,000
Georgia Bank, robbed by Baker	80,000
Frederick (Maryland) Bank, compromised by Bill Wiley	186,000
Norwich Railroad, by the president	10,000
Bank of Louisiana, by the teller	60,000
Bank of Orleans, by the teller	80,000
Canal Bank of New Orleans, by the teller	100,000
Bank of Michigan, by the officers	100,000
State Bank of Illinois, by town	90,000
Merchants' Bank of Baltimore, by clerk	10,000
Tennessee Bank, Nashville, by officers	7,000
Frankfort Bank, by the president	100,000
State Bank of Arkansas, by Ball	64,000
Twenty-three New York banks, by officers	1,500,000
Pennsylvania Bank, by officer, Smith	100,000
Western Bank, by cashier, Israel	15,000
Camden New Jersey Bank, by Patterson	13,000
Farmers' Bank (Troy), by Jones	10,000
Western Bank (Georgia), by Moore	75,000
Bank of Cape Fear (North Carolina), by cashier	10,000
Bank of Wooster (Ohio), by officers	100,000
Planters' Bank (Georgia), by officers	105,000
Bank of Steubenville (Ohio), by officers	125,000
Forward	$39,790,000

TABLE I—*Continued*

Brought forward	$39,790,000
Franklin Bank, Baltimore, by Stanberger	50,000
Newbury Port Bank, by Wychoff	30,000
Willington Bank (Maryland), by Sherwood . . .	50,000
Gallipolis Bank (Ohio), by officers	20,000
Ten other Ohio banks, by officers	1,000,000
Six Maine banks, by officers	800,000
Herkimer County Bank, by clerks	72,000
Commercial Bank (New York), by officers (one-half the capital)	250,000
Forgeries of Mitchell, Smith, and numerous others	200,000
	$42,262,000

The report continues:

This is but a portion of the amount swindled. It is impossible to ascertain the amounts lost by counterfeits, depreciation, etc. Bicknell, in the same year (1839), ascertained that counterfeits on 254 different banks were in circulation, and enumerated 1,395 descriptions of counterfeited or altered notes then supposed to be in circulation, of denominations from one to five hundred dollars.[1]

The natural consequence of these actions was the loss of confidence and the destruction of the moral feeling of obligation. The suspension of the banks was first tolerated and then legalized.

The banks set the example in breaking through the moral obligation of indebtedness by refusing to pay their debts, and the legislature sanctioned it. From this the transition was easy to a suspension of bank debtors, particularly where, as in Alabama, the state was the creditor in the form

[1] *Illinois Senate House Reports*, II (1842), 191–93.

of the bank. Debts were accordingly extended several years, and money borrowed to lend embarrassed debtors. The next step was to protect debtors from individual creditors. The usury laws were taken advantage of unblushingly.

States passed stay and valuation laws "which deprived the creditor of the power, under state laws, of collecting his claims. The next movement was to scrutinize the manner in which state debts had been contracted, and repudiation to avoid taxation was the result." As the clamor for relief gained momentum, "the federal administration was changed under the promise of a bankrupt law, to absolve individuals from their debts; of a distribution of the public lands, to relieve the state; of a national bank, to afford supposed relief to trade generally; and of a high tariff, to relieve manufacturers." The bankrupt law was enacted, and "thirty thousand individuals with aggregate debts estimated at $2,000,000, or about $7,000 each, were exonerated from their liabilities." The distribution law was repealed, because the threatened bankruptcy of the federal government required it, while the political situation made impossible the passage of a new one. Thus, as *Hunt's Merchants' Magazine* announced in 1843:

All those moral and legal obligations which formed the basis of credit have been swept away. A merchant cannot trust a western dealer, because the state laws give him no protection. The capitalist cannot repose confidence in banks, because, monthly and weekly for the past three years,

explosions have taken place disclosing fraud and misman-
agement of the most astounding nature. Upwards of sixty
banks have failed, sinking $132,363,800 of capital. He cannot
trust states, because the same principles which induced the
passage of stay laws disposed the people to resist taxation.
Investments in property, real and personal, have been
dangerous, because [of] the increasing discredit, the contraction of the currency attending the failure of the banks has
caused prices continually to recede, and in falling markets
no one is prone to operate.[1]

Various estimates of the havoc wrought by the
panic appeared in diverse forms. A writer of a
series of papers published in New York in 1840,
entitled *Letters to the People of the United States by
Concivis*, showing a great deal of ability and apparent labor of investigation, sums up a catalogue of the
losses in the whole country for the period 1837–41
(Table II).

TABLE II[2]

Losses in wool	$ 20,000,000
Losses in cotton	130,000,000
Losses in grain	150,000,000
Losses in foreign merchandise	130,000,000
Losses in domestic merchandise	400,000,000
Losses in capital vested in manufactures	50,000,000
Losses of capital vested in moneyed stocks	150,000,000
Losses in capital vested in slave labor	400,000,000
Losses in capital vested in lands	2,500,000,000
Losses in capital vested in real estate in cities	500,000,000
Losses on price of labor	1,500,000,000

[1] *Hunt's Merchants' Magazine*, VIII, 272, 273.

[2] Colton, *Life and Times of Clay*, II, 66.

Another attempt to state the losses from 1837 to 1841 was set forth by the *United States Almanac* (Table III).

TABLE III*

Losses on banks' circulation and deposits....	$ 54,000,000
Losses on capital failed and depreciated......	100,000,000
Losses on state stock, depreciated..........	100,000,000
Losses on company stocks.................	80,000,000
Losses on real estate.....................	300,000,000

* Colton, *Life and Times of Clay*, II, 66.

A third approximation of the general devastation was advanced by the grand committee of New York, which waited on President Van Buren in the height of the panic, asking for relief. These men affirmed the following conditions to be true:

That the value of their real estate had, within the last six months, depreciated more than $40,000,000; that within the last two months there had been more than 250 failures of houses engaged in extensive business; that within the same period a decline of $20,000,000 had occurred in their local stocks, including those railroad and canal corporations which, though chartered in other states, depended chiefly on New York for their sales; and that the immense amount of merchandise in their warehouses had within the same period fallen in value at least 30 per cent.[1]

Still later, Juglar trying to estimate the enormous loss, asserted that "according to some pretty accurate reports in 1841, 33,000 failures, involving a loss of $440,000,000," had developed from the panic.[2]

[1] Benton, *Thirty Years' View*, II, 18.

[2] Juglar, *A Brief History of Panics*, p. 80.

When we remember, however, that all these figures are merely estimates, but that all except those given by the last-mentioned authority are by persons living during these years, these statistics assume their proper proportion. They are contemporary evidence of what the people of those days thought about the panic, and show us that to them the figures must be in the hundreds of millions to attempt to gauge the terrible havoc.

Government statistics for these years are also interesting. The imports between 1836 and 1838 show a drop of $49,000,000 in value, most of which was in cotton goods, silk goods, linen, iron, steel, sugar, teas, and wines.[1] In like manner, the exports illustrate a great decline between 1836 and 1838, the chief falling-off being in cotton, tobacco, and rice. New York and Louisiana were the chief regions affected. A similar decrease in the land sales is evidenced by the fact that in 1837 the sales fell under $7,000,000, and in the first three quarters of 1838 a little more than $2,000,000.[2]

The most significant results of the panic were the marked westward movement, the stimulus given to railroads, and the redistribution of wealth.[3] The westward movement was quickly sensed by the

[1] *Hunt's Merchants' Magazine*, I, 184.

[2] Trotter, *op. cit.*, pp. 46–49, 383, 384.

[3] On the redistribution of wealth, cf. Scott, *Repudiation of State Debts*, pp. 227, 228.

people of these days. A Boston newspaper of April 14, 1837, said: "The emigration to the great west is rapidly increasing from different parts of the country. The present stagnation in business and the disastrous effect . . . . upon our mechanics and laborers . . . . will tend to send many of them from our large towns and cities, where their services have been in constant demand for some years."[1] Thus the poor people, "lacking the means of support in their native cities, took up the heritage of the poor man, cheap lands in a new country."[2]

Besides this, the railroads received an added impulse from the crisis. Canals which had been projected on speculation and state aid fell in the crash that came during these years. Naturally a certain degree of odium attached to them as the result of their failure. On the other hand, the railroads which had been planned were so few in number in comparison with the canals that their failure did not attract much attention. Moreover, since the canals were gone, and as some means of communication was necessary, the railroads found themselves in better repute than heretofore. As a result the necessity of new railroads became apparent.[3]

[1] *Boston Mercantile Journal*, quoted in *Chicago Weekly American*, May 6, 1837.

[2] Pooley, *op. cit.*, p. 335.

[3] Hadley, *Railroad Transportation*, p. 33.

Another important result of the financial and industrial unrest was its effect upon the politics of the day. The Whig party and the Biddle men saw their opportunity to regain their lost prestige in the labor unrest during these years. Straightway the old struggle between the banks and the government was resumed, to be fought out once more at the ballot box and in Congress. The economic hardships between 1837 and 1840 conditioned the lines of attack, and foretold the ultimate outcome. It gave the Whigs a rallying cry; it enabled Biddle to strive for power; it brought on a definite clash between labor and capital; and it prepared the way for the long struggle over the Sub-treasury measure, the most important bill of the Van Buren administration.

CHAPTER V

POLITICAL AFTERMATH OF
THE PANIC

When the condition of the patient is truly alarming, and the physician's skill is baffled by the disease, quacks gain confidence by their boldness and boasting.—

BIDDLE PAPERS

The panic of 1837 loosened the political moorings of the thirties. For eight years—from 1828 to 1836—the Democratic party was the dominant party in the nation. For eight years it weathered the storms of nullification, bank, tariff, internal improvements, speculations, and foreign affairs. But the commercial crisis of 1837 was to seal its doom. The long-pent-up emotions of the people, the discordant clashing of capital and labor, the rival aspirations of party leaders, and the last phase of the struggle between "bank and the state" were to find their outlet in the money stringency. To Van Buren, the successor of Jackson, was left the handling of these manifold questions. To him remained the burden of proof that the Democratic administrations had not caused these evils.

The Democrats fully realized their dilemma. They appreciated the fact that at last their opponents had a battle cry, and would use it to advantage in the coming elections. By April of 1837 the President began to receive letters from his associates expressing anxiety about the political prospects of the party.[1] In May came evidence of the defection within the party, the lack of organization and incentive, the wearisomeness of the public mind with the long strife, and the determination of the opposition to turn the panic to political account.[2] Urgent appeals poured into the White House for relief, until at last, on May 15, Van Buren issued his proclamation for an extra session to meet on the first Monday of September. It would meet, the proclamation stated, to consider "great and weighty matters"; and the Democratic party leaders apprehended that their salvation rested upon the work of this congress. "The next step we take as a party," wrote Buchanan to Van Buren, "in relation to public revenue, if it should not be successful, will prostrate us and re-establish the Bank of the United States. . . . . The new experiment, whatever it may be, must succeed in order to preserve the people's approbation."[3] "The opposition anticipate great success in the present difficulties," reiterated the *Globe*.

[1] Mann to Van Buren, April 3, 1837; Toland to Van Buren, April 3, 1837; Rives to Van Buren, April 7, 1837, Van Buren MSS.

[2] Wright to Van Buren, May 13, 1837, and numerous others in Van Buren MSS.

[3] Buchanan to Van Buren, June 6, 1837, Van Buren MSS.

"They know that there is a diversity of opinion among the Republicans as regards the utility of banking institutions, and hope to extend this difference to a question wholly independent, which involves simply the propriety of banking connection with the government."[1] Calhoun also noted the divergence of opinion among the Democratic followers, and prophesied a like division through all the states. At the same time, Ritchie wrote to friends of the lowering storm which was coming.[2] Throughout the summer months the popular excitement swelled against the administration. The Whig papers, such as the *National Intelligencer*, proclaimed the issue before the people was whether this was "to be a government of state banks and paper credit, or a government of the people," and other papers pointed out "the melancholy truth, the awful truth, that the administration did nothing to relieve the distress."[3]

On September 4, 1837, Van Buren read his message to Congress and advised the creation of an Independent Treasury to care for the finances of the government. At once a storm of protest arose on all sides. In Virginia but one press defended the Sub-treasury scheme. Many of the most influential

[1] *Globe*, July 21, 1837.

[2] Jameson, *Correspondence of Calhoun*, pp. 377, 378; Ambler, *Thomas Ritchie*, p. 190.

[3] *National Intelligencer*, June 2, 1837.

Democratic papers in the Union, "among which the *Richmond Enquirer*, the *Hartford Patriot*, the *Frederick [Maryland] Times*, and the *Cincinnati Republican* considered the system unwise and inexpedient."[1] Immediately a section of the Democratic party under the leadership of Nathaniel P. Tallmadge, of New York, and William C. Rives, of Virginia, broke with the President. Candidates were called upon for their opinions on the Subtreasury bill, while the diversity of thought on the subject continued to grow in the Democratic ranks. Dr. Thomas Cooper, writing to Biddle on the fifteenth, prophesied a seven years' war between the government and the banks, and the ultimate conversion into a regular contest between the agricultural and "the moneyed, or mercantile, interests." "We are yet at the commencement of the great strife," continued the writer, "and I think there are strong indications that the numerical majority of the people are hostile to all banks."[2]

With the projection of the Sub-treasury into the political arena, Van Buren had appealed to the people for a complete divorce of state and bank. Throughout his whole administration, in the state elections and in Congress, this question was to be uppermost, and upon it was to rest the fate of the Whig and Democratic parties, the relation of

[1] *New York Times*, October 3, 1837.

[2] Cooper to Biddle, September 15, 1837, B.P.

capital and labor, the fate of a national bank, and the career of Nicholas Biddle. By using the commercial crisis and the Sub-treasury plan as weapons, the Whigs were to mount to power; and an examination of the state elections from 1837 to 1840 discloses this titanic struggle between bank and government for supremacy.

The contest between capital and labor received definite origin in the state of New York in 1834. In that year there was founded the young, vigorous, honest, and patriotic, but quixotic, indiscreet, and injudicious Locofoco party. At the close of the spring election it was seen that the Whig and Democratic parties were evenly balanced. Both resolved to work for an increase in their members in order to secure a victory in the next election. A very large portion in the Democratic party, who had assisted the President in his efforts to overthrow the Bank of the United States, naturally inferred that they were engaged in a war against all banks and all monopolies. Yet it was apparent, "notwithstanding that great caution was used to conceal the fact," that many regular Democrats were hostile to such a plan. But the crisis was too imminent to exhibit their sentiment, and so, perhaps due to bargaining among themselves, they agreed to postpone their opposition until after the November election. Accordingly, they pledged themselves to oppose all monopolies, and so united the Democratic party was again victorious with greatly increased majorities. Once in power, the Bank Democrats repudiated their pledges, poured ridicule and contempt upon their former promises, and in a variety of ways endeavored to burlesque and insult those who with "honesty and zeal worked to carry into effect the will of the people." This injustice rankled in the minds of the mechanics and laborers of the party. Then came the historic meeting of October 29, 1835, when the anti-monopolistic Democrats received the cognomen of "Locofoco." Thus was formed a party of "mechanics and laborers believing in free trade, equal rights for all men, opposition to all bank notes and paper money as circulating medium, and to all forms of exclusive privilege." Their political philosophy found expression in the writings of such men as George H. Evans, William Leggett, and William Cullen Bryant,[1] and was welcomed with as great horror as their kinsmen, the Chartists, were later accorded in England. But at last labor had found an organization to combat capital, and as such became a factor in state politics.

The advent of the new party into New York politics was welcomed with mingled feelings of

[1] The story of the origin of the Locofoco party is well told in the *New York Evening Post*, September 19, 1837. Cf. also *The Man passim; New York Journal of Commerce* for 1835; Byrdsall, *History of Locofocos, or Equal Rights Party;* Trimble, "Diverging Tendencies in New York Democracy in the Period of the Locofocos," in *Amer. Hist. Rev.*, April, 1919, pp. 396–422.

alarm and joy by the Whigs; alarm lest these "Jack
Cades"[1] should arouse the agrarian spirit throughout the nation; joy that the Democratic ranks
would be divided. Even though the Locofocos
boldly proclaimed they were reformers but still
Democrats, maintaining a position of independence
toward both parties, they served best the Whig
organization. By dividing the votes within the
city, they enabled the Whigs to secure a footing.
The fall elections of 1835 demonstrated this, and
largely owing to their efforts, the Whigs elected
their candidate as mayor in the spring of 1837. No
one imagined that a political revolution was imminent, but the suffering people were angry, and in the
fall elections of 1837 they were to play an important
part. Whig and Democratic leaders watched with
anxiety their party organization in New York as the
time for the election approached. Van Buren received frequent information of the split among the
Democrats, due to the presence of Bank Democrats
and Locofocos. He was warned that the Locofocos
would sooner see the Democratic party scattered to
the four winds than give up their favorite notions;
that this was particularly true of their leaders; but
that the great mass of the party was honest, and

---

[1] Colt to Biddle, August 5, 1837; Coryell to Biddle, July 14,
1837; Thayer to Biddle, May 3, 1837, B.P. The correspondents of
Biddle often referred to this party as one of "Jack Cades, Agrari-
ans, and Fanny Wrighters." Consult also Marcy to Wetmore,
July 12, 1837; Marcy to Gallup, September 23, 1837, Marcy MSS.

ready to do what was right, and if proper measures were pursued they might be brought back into good fellowship with the Democratic party.[1] On the other hand, Biddle watched with fear this new rising of labor opposed to all banks and special privileges, and the Whig press hurled anathema after anathema at the Equal Righters.

At last appeared Van Buren's message to Congress. The sky at once cleared. The bank conservatives broke with the President, and the Locofocos split among themselves. The message was received with acclaim by the Locofocos, because, if it did not place Van Buren in an attitude of "war against the banks, it at all events placed the banks in a belligerent attitude toward him." The division within Tammany prepared the way for a reconciliation; negotiations were opened up, and it soon became apparent that members of "Slam Bang & Company" (as the Locofocos were sometimes called) were to be received with open arms into the fold of the Tammany organization. A cry of horror arose from the old regular Democrats. They refused to acquiesce in this new arrangement; they proclaimed against the spirit of destruction which the Locofocos advocated; and they openly declared against Van Buren as a new convert to the Equal Rights organization.

[1] Bates to Van Buren, May 25, 1837, V.B. MSS; *Plaindealer*, April 22, 1837.

The diverging tendencies in the New York Democracy, so ably described by Professor Trimble, became apparent.[1] The new adherents appealed to the fountain of Democracy for sanctification—President Jackson—thus:

We who address you, sir, are attached and belong to the party pledged to the name and principles of Equal Rights ever since its first ostensible formation in the fall of 1835. We then took our stand, not more than sixteen-hundred strong, equally against the Whig or old Federalist enemy and the regular Democratic party, so-called. But now the situation has changed. The noble message of your worthy successor has operated powerfully upon the public mind. Men who formerly had allowed their principles to be swept away by the tide of demoralizing circumstances, and who saw no haven for which to make . . . . now rally to the voice of the National Pilot. . . . . Under these circumstances, we of the extreme reformers . . . . are disposed to hope and believe that from this time forward—more especially since the purging of the Democratic party by the succession [secession] of the conservatives—the ranks of the *people* may again blend with those of the ostensible administrative party. . . . . The whole of our party, perhaps, at this time numbers five thousand votes. Let these all unite on one ticket with the true division of old Tammany, and we think that our city will be saved.[2]

The sanction was given; the Locofoco party entered the Tammany wigwam.

[1] Cf. Trimble, *op. cit.*, in *Amer. Hist. Rev.*, April, 1919.

[2] Appeal of Equal Righters to Jackson, October 3(?), 1837. Jackson MSS. This appeal is indorsed by Jackson, in his own handwriting, as follows: "My farewell address to the American

Tammany's seeming acceptance of Locofoco principles played into the hands of their opponents. The Whigs were overjoyed at the confusion reigning in the Democratic ranks. The Whig organs seized upon this union of the Democrats and Locofocos to widen the breach in the Democratic party in New York. "The fact is clear that the people of New York are not Locofocos," proclaimed the *National Intelligencer*. "A reasonable degree of equality they have no objection to; but Locofocoism strikes at bed and board, colors and races, property and persons." The purpose of the Whig leaders was to fix definitely upon the whole Democratic organization of the state this hated epithet. In this they succeeded. The Democratic ranks were torn asunder; the conservatives joined the Whigs in their cry against the rights of labor; regular Democrats, such as Governor Marcy, found it difficult to stand by the administration and the state organization, now that the Locofocos had become "mighty men" in the party, according to a letter by the Governor to a friend:

The insolence of the Locofocos . . . . is almost insufferable, and operated powerfully to create and confirm our

---

people fully, if attended to, warns the Republican party of the necessities of union to protect their government from the devices of the Federalist party, whose aim is to divide the Republican party by specious decrees, and conquer them, and lastly to govern the democratic members by the money power welded by the aristocracy of the few—refer to this address—you have my views."

threatened divisions. They regard themselves as the fathers of the church, and even Mr. V.B. is only one of their recent converts. Is it reasonable to expect that the Democrats of the state will range themselves under the banners of Ming, Leggett, Slam Jaques, and others of better repute at Washington, but not more deserving. . . . . The doctrines of the day are essentially destructive. . . . . The cry is up against the banks, and they must be surrendered to the hideous monster of Locofocoism.[1]

The prospects of the party were gloomy; and as the discontent spread, the Democratic leaders, forgetting the principles upon which their party was founded, became autocratic. This tendency was deprecated by the Democratic *New York Times:*

There are too many who tolerate no freedom of opinion, but would excommunicate at once all brethren who assent not promptly to their views, by what means, or how recently soever they came by them themselves. . . . . He is a seceder who goes not for the Sub-treasury. . . . . He is a Democrat who goes for it, though he were a Whig or Locofoco yesterday. . . . . Who doubts is damned. The President has suggested the scheme. Why do they not register his will at once and so "support him" like good Democrats? That is Republicanism now; and the people are sovereign and independent no longer. They have elected a president to think for them.[2]

The election verified the Democratic fears. The Whigs campaigned on the money stringency, Locofocoism, and agrarianism. Biddle sent money (but

[1] Marcy to Gallup, September 23, 1837, Marcy MSS.

[2] *New York Times*, quoted in *Philadelphia Daily Gazette*, October 2, 1837.

unwillingly) to his cousin to carry on the contest,
and the bank Conservatives, allied with the Whigs,
were credited "with raising an election fund of
$60,000."[1] The result was easily foreseen. New
York State, which the year before had given Van
Buren a plurality of nearly thirty thousand, wheeled
into the Whig ranks. They carried the assembly by
121 to 27, and elected ten out of the twenty-two
senators.[2] Some of the strongest Democratic counties gave Whig returns, and some of the Democrats
even refused to vote upon election day. When one
stops to consider the strength of the Democratic
party in New York before the crisis, the magnitude
of the achievement is amazing.

In Massachusetts the outcome of the struggle
was similar to New York. The issue in the election
was bank or anti-bank, and about these two words
the two parties rallied. The Whigs raised a "hue
and cry" about the suffering of the "mercantile
community," the laboring classes deprived of "the
benefits of their industry," and the depression and
bankruptcy of the manufacturers. The power of the
panic remained unbroken. A Whig majority was
registered, and the party went into ecstasies over
their continued good fortune.[3]

[1] McGrane, *op. cit.*, p. 292; Myers, *History of Tammany Hall*,
p. 135.

[2] Niles, November 25, 1837.

[3] *Worcester Republican*, October 25, 1837; *Lowell Courier*,
November 11, 1837.

The other New England states presented corresponding reversals of feeling. Maine, the stronghold of the administration, fell in line with her sister states. "Maine is essentially a commercial state, and all its interests are more or less connected with trade"; therefore the reason for the Whig gain was easily explained, said the *New York Daily News*. Van Buren's message, the split in the Democratic ranks, the culpable negligence of Democratic voters in not going to the polls, were also cited as causes; but the confession on the part of the *New York Daily News* was seized upon with avidity by the Whig leaders in explaining the situation.[1] Rhode Island followed in the footsteps of Maine. The change in public feeling, the opposition within Democratic folds, the apathy of Democratic voters, the property qualifications for voting, and the fear of Locofoco principles, were all given as explanations for the defeat. But the laconic statement of the Whig *Boston Chronicle and Patriot*, that the result "affords a striking proof of the effects of the disastrous policy of the government," typified the victors' view of the contest.[2] Vermont likewise registered a Whig majority.[3] It was only in the

---

[1] *New York Daily News*, quoted in *Philadelphia Advertiser*, September 23, 1837.

[2] Mallett to Van Buren, July 17, 1837, Van Buren MSS; *Baltimore Republican*, September 2, 1837; *The Man*, September 6, 1837; *Boston Chronicle and Patriot*, September 2, 1837.

[3] *Vermont Argus*, September 12, 1837.

middle section, in the state of Pennsylvania, that the Democrats received any consolation in their hour of deepest humiliation. Here the opposition to the United States Bank of Pennsylvania aided their cause. Notwithstanding the fact that Biddle was well informed of the "need of pecuniary assistance," and the Biddleites honestly fought hard, the people showed their opposition in an unmistakable manner.[1]

Meanwhile, the questions of Sub-treasury and capital versus labor were convulsing the southern elections. Van Buren's stand against abolition and Calhoun's return to the Democratic party benefited materially the administration party. In Virginia, Rives and his followers joined the northern Conservatives; in South Carolina, Calhoun reversed his former position and re-entered the party. Jackson bemoaned the terrible condition of Tennessee politics; Georgia began to drift from the administration ranks; Mississippi showed signs of changing its political complexion; on all sides the southern states presented a disheartened appearance to the Democratic leaders.[2]

But the whole South was not to surrender unconditionally to the Whig organization. Two factors were to prevent this: first, the Democratic

[1] Reed to Biddle, September 12, 1837; Smith to Biddle, September 27, 1837, B.P.

[2] Jackson to Blair, August 16, 1837, Jackson MSS; Phillips, *Georgia and State Rights*, p. 145; Bolton to Curtis, May 5, 1837, New York and Mississippi Land Company MSS.

party was too well rooted in the South to be ousted so easily; secondly, "King Cotton" wished to safeguard his interests, as well as "King Capital." As the shrewd Pickens diagnosed the situation, the great struggle was "whether cotton shall control exchanges and importations, or whether the banks and the stock interests shall do it." The great issue was made up; the war was between capitalists in stock and corporations, and capital in labor and lands, as Pickens wrote to Hammond:

The struggle is for ascendency, and if the former are sustained in their swindling career they will control and own the latter. I go for land and negroes. Break down the swindling of bankers, and the capitalists of the South will control the confederacy, drive out, to a great extent, paper credits, except upon bona fide capital, and cotton will do the exchanges of the commercial world. . . . . The capitalists of the North have by their corporations concentrated their power as in one man. We are already organized, and the fundamental principle of our society is that we own the labor of the country. We have never had their sympathy, and they do not deserve ours when their system has received a shock and they are brought to the edge of bankruptcy and ruin. The South will be more prosperous under cotton at ten cents, and no banks connected with the government, lending its credit and power to the stock interest, than we would be under the latter at thirteen cents, and the reverse of these things.[1]

The state elections demonstrated these points. In Mississippi the Whigs pleaded the pressure,

[1] Pickens to Hammond, July 13, 1837, Hammond MSS.

abused the Specie Circular, condemned the veto of the United States Bank and every other measure of the Jacksonian administration, to no purpose.[1] With corresponding exasperation, Alabama disappointed the hopes of the opponents of the administration.[2] But in both cases it ought to be borne in mind that the elections were held early in the year, when the full effects of the panic and the Sub-treasury had not begun their insidious work. In Georgia, however, the Democratic papers openly acknowledged that their defeat was due to the "commercial embarrassments of the country" and the Sub-treasury bill.[3] North Carolina and Maryland helped swell the Whig victories with their returns, much to the rage of ex-President Jackson.[4] "The disordered condition of the currency" proved an effective weapon in the commercial cities of the latter state (as, in fact, in all states), and as Taney remarked later to Jackson, the money power was irresistible:

It is not by open corruption that it always, or even most generally, operates. But when men who have families to support, who depend for bread upon their exertions, are aware that on one side they will be employed and enriched by those who have the power to distribute wealth, and that if they take the other they must struggle with every difficulty that

[1] *Richmond Enquirer*, August 29, 1837.

[2] *Philadelphia Advertiser*, August 5, 1837.

[3] *National Intelligencer*, October 26, 1837.

[4] Niles, October 7, 1837.

can be thrown in their way, they are very apt to persuade themselves that that path is the best in which they meet the fewest difficulties and most favor, and surrender the lasting blessings of freedom and manly independence for temporary pecuniary advantages.[1]

In the West the Whigs swept everything before them in their march to victory. The governor of Illinois, in his message of July, intimated that perhaps the "experiments" might have a political effect. His fears were substantiated in the fall elections. A spirit of unrest seemed to pervade the West as a consequence of the hard times, and the people demanded a change. True, their condition was not as bad, in 1837, as in certain other districts, but they had not entirely escaped the holocaust and therefore they were resolved to hold the administration accountable for the distress. Indiana and Kentucky registered Whig victories. As for Tennessee, the actions of Bell, the supineness of the Democratic leaders, the energy of their opponents, and the prominence of the Sub-treasury placed the state in the Whig columns.[2] In Ohio the Whigs elected sixty-two members to the assembly as against forty-eight by the Democrats. The *Cincinnati Republican*, presumably a Van Buren paper, but actuated by conservative principles, was

---

[1] Taney to Jackson, September 12, 1838, Jackson MSS. This letter, although written in 1838, is correct for the elections of 1837.

[2] Jackson to Blair, August 16, 1837, Jackson MSS.

blamed for the actions of the voters. It was asserted that no less than 1,900 Democratic voters had declined voting, owing to the hollow-hearted maneuvers of the Republican.[1] The apostasy of the Democratic press, the vigor of their rivals' papers, and the cry of hard times gave the Whigs large majorities in the western states. "It is well known," announced the *Philadelphia Advertiser*, "to be a difficult business to induce the farmers to leave the beaten paths of their fathers and grandfathers, except in times of imminent danger."

By December the fall elections were completed, and the two parties were able to survey the results. According to the Whig almanac they stood as shown in Table IV. Nevertheless, Van Buren refused to be discouraged with the outcome, while on the other hand the Whigs were over-jubilant. The Sub-treasury had not received a warm welcome from the people. By means of the division caused by this measure, and the apathy within the Democratic folds, and the money stringency, the Whigs had made tremendous strides within the nation. The New England section and the West revealed increased majorities, and only in the South, where the Federalists' power encountered the planters' interests and states' rights, had their path been impeded. The interests of Van Buren and Nicholas Biddle had clashed, and so far the people had sided with the

[1] Dawson to Jackson, December 4, 1837, Jackson MSS.

bank party. The strife between labor and capital, state and bank, had revolutionized the political aspects of the nation; but, as yet, nothing had been settled. Neither side was satisfied; both were determined to go once more before the people in the coming elections of 1838.

TABLE IV*

State	Democrat	Whig
Maine.....................	33,971	34,513
Vermont....................	17,730	22,260
Connecticut................	23,805	21,508
Massachusetts..............	32,987	59,595
Rhode Island...............	3,261	4,282
New Jersey.................	24,856	27,368
Pennsylvania...............	91,182	85,890
Maryland (about)...........	23,000	25,000
New York...................	140,460	155,883
North Carolina (about)......	30,000	35,000
Georgia....................	29,415	30,160
Alabama....................	26,133	20,551
Mississippi................	11,203	7,631
Kentucky...................	23,955	47,415
Tennessee..................	33,606	53,479
Indiana....................	28,125	53,867
Michigan...................	10,705	9,594
Arkansas...................	nearly balanced	....

* *Whig Almanac*, 1837; *Philadelphia Daily Gazette*, May 3, 1838. No returns for Ohio.

New York was still the pivotal state in politics, as it was in financial matters. Naturally, the Whigs put forth every effort to carry the state, quell the rising claims of labor, and defeat the administration. If only the Conservatives and Locofocos would continue their Kilkenny strife, Biddle was assured

the Whigs would win.[1] Nevertheless, the charter
elections in the spring proved discouraging to the
opponents of the government, as it revealed un-
expected harmony and organization among the
Democrats.[2] Many prophesied that the fall elections would result in the defeat of the Whigs by a
majority of six or ten thousand, that the regency
was not as profligate as the Whigs represented them,
and that prospects were undoubtedly bright. "The
only way to defeat the administration is to push forward the Locofocos," wrote Davis to Biddle, "the
more Locofoco the nominations, the better for
us." Again the Whigs intended to raise the cry
against the "levelers," apply the epithet to the
whole Democratic régime, and, aided by the "embarrassed commerce and crippled manufactures,"
turn the tide for the Whigs. Boldly urging the restoration of the currency, commerce, prosperity, and
tranquillity, proclaiming against the doctrines of
the Equal Righters and the Sub-treasury, and calling
upon the people to hold their candidates accountable for their votes in Congress, the Whigs
maintained their hold, but at greatly reduced
majorities.[3] Once more capital had overcome labor
on the plea of the extravagance of Locofoco principles.

[1] Davis to Biddle, March 15, 1838, B.P.

[2] Butler to Van Buren, April 17, 1838, Van Buren MSS.

[3] Seward, *Autobiography*, I, 374.

Marcy, in a letter to a friend, summarized the Democratic explanation for the defeat of 1838.

As I do not intend that what I shall write shall be seen by any eyes but yours and mine, you must not expect a labored effort; but you may, however, expect that I shall speak with great frankness, and say many things that would be indiscreet if they were intended to be thrown before the public at this time. . . . . The election was conducted chiefly with reference to the policy of the federal government. If we had had nothing but our own policy to vindicate, I cannot bring myself to doubt that we should have had a different result.

Then, referring to the old strife with the United States Bank, the governor pointed out that in this warfare they "had an efficient ally in the state institutions, and it seemed unwise to enter into a war with this power, so recently a useful ally, while the old enemy which it aided us to conquer had scattered forces which could be rallied and brought into the field in the consuming engagement." This statement he proceeds to amplify:

It is undoubtedly true as a general abstract proposition that wealth is hostile to democracy. The possession of the former engenders, in weak and ordinary minds, contempt for the latter. We should be blind not to see that the mass of influence of moneyed institutions will, under ordinary circumstances, be swayed against the Democratic party. . . . . The measures of the general government have been such as to enlist the power of money against the Democratic party to a greater extent than has ever happened before.

Moreover, the prominence given to the Loco-focos, together with the abhorrence "felt for their ultra-leveling doctrines," alarmed the business interests of the state. This, in time, "opened the purses of our political opponents, and thereby gave rise to the enormous 'corruption fund' which was so efficiently used against us":

> Direct bribery constituted but a small part of the mischief which the use of this corruption fund has inflicted upon us. It has set agents to work in every section of the state, who have used deception, coercion, and double voting. . . . . Money has corrupted some, it has set agents to work who have deceived others, it has prompted exertions by which thousands have been brought to the polls, who otherwise would not have attended the elections; it surrounded the polls with bullies; it not only stimulated the tools of the opposition to extraordinary activity, but induced them to resort to unfair and high-handed means.

Finally, the suppression of the small bills operated against the Democrats in the country, where the people needed a safe medium of exchange, and the adroit alliance of Abolitionists with the Whigs completed the list of causes explaining the Democratic defeat.[1]

In Massachusetts, the Democrats made the Sub-treasury the main issue. "The great question involved in the coming election is," declared the

[1] Marcy to Wetmore, August 16, 23, 1838; Worth to Marcy, October 16, 1838; Marcy to Wetmore, December 11, 1838, Marcy MSS.

Worcester Palladium, "whether we shall have a government independent of banks, or one that is the mere agent of associated wealth, that will consult the interests of capital to the preference of labor." Candidates were selected on both sides with reference to the financial policy of the government, but the Whigs still controlled the state, although at a reduced majority.[1] Maine, however, wheeled back into the Van Buren column.[2] In New Hampshire the opponents of the administration succeeded in electing their man to the governorship by a large majority, and placed a number in the House. "Granite states don't change front of a sudden, but this is a violent wheel," exultantly announced the *National Intelligencer.*[3] As a consequence of the hard times of 1837 and the division in the Democratic ranks, Connecticut acted in a similar fashion.[4] In Pennsylvania the contest raged with increasing bitterness. Here Governor Ritner was defeated by Porter, the Democratic candidate for governor, by a majority of more than one thousand. Ritner's action in connection with the recharter of the Bank, the opposition of the farmers to all banks, and the

---

[1] *Worcester Palladium,* November 7, 1838; *Worcester Republican,* November 21, 1838.

[2] *Lowell Courier,* September 22, 1838; *Albany Argus,* September 25, 1838.

[3] *National Intelligencer,* March 22, 27, 1838.

[4] Niles, April 14, 1838.

fact that Biddle would not help in the campaign
contributed to the downfall of the Whig supremacy.[1] In truth, the eastern elections looked as
though a counter-reformation had taken place.
The appeal of the Whigs based on the panic was
losing its force, and only where the Sub-treasury was
specially prominent and the Whigs could employ
the cry of Locofocoism did the party seem secure.[2]

The Sub-treasury program and the hardships
wrought by the panic proved more effective in the
southern elections of this year. With the exception
of Maryland, Alabama, and South Carolina, the
Whigs had cause to rejoice in the future prospects of
their party in this section.[3] The cotton-growing
counties of Mississippi came to the support of the
Whig party, with the result that a Whig majority
was returned in both branches of the legislature.[4] In
North Carolina the Whigs united in opposition to the
Sub-treasury, and with this as their slogan, carried
the state.[5] Georgia continued along the line she had
set down in 1837, showing an increasing opposition

[1] Fraley to Biddle, March 24, 1838; Penrose to Biddle, July
13, 1838; Blatchford to Biddle, October 17, 1838, B.P.

[2] *Albany Argus*, October 30, 1838.

[3] *Albany Journal*, October 8, 12, 1838; *National Intelligencer*
October 9, 31, 1838.

[4] *National Intelligencer*, June 12, 16, 1838.

[5] *Albany Argus*, August 15, 1838; *Albany Journal*, August 20,
1838.

to Van Buren and the Sub-treasury measure.[1] But the best examples of Whig gains by "panic methods" were evidenced in Virginia and Louisiana. In 1838 the breach in the Democratic ranks in Virginia was most pronounced, and the petty jealousies of certain members among the Democrats were kept afire by the vigilant opposition. The ever watchful Ritchie bemoaned, in the *Richmond Enquirer*, the aspect of affairs:

The country is distressed, and the sole blame of it has been laid at the door of the administration. Our party has been never more distracted, torn to pieces in many counties, wrangling with each other, unwilling to co-operate, and many of them would not go to the polls. We have fought amid suspension and shin plasters, amid the discords of Sub-treasury and conservative. An extraordinary apathy has pervaded many of our counties. In several of them, no organization—two or three candidates running against each other, as if such a competition would mend the matter— whilst, in one of the most Republican counties, not even a Republican candidate was in the field. . . . . All we want is harmony and peace. Let the finance question be settled at Washington.[2]

Again, in a letter which he wrote to Van Buren, dated July 2, 1838, he reiterated his fears. "I beg you in the most emphatic terms to close up this most vexatious question [subtreasury] now. . . . . I pray you not to listen to those infuriated bitter

[1] *New York Evening Star*, October 19, 1838; Phillips, *op. cit.*, p. 140.

[2] Quoted in the *Globe*, May 2, 1838.

hotspurs who advise you to appeal to the polls. Before the fall elections, the schism in our party may produce the direst results." But the warning of Ritchie went unheeded, and the Whigs carried the state in the spring of 1838.[1]

In another state in the South the effect of the panic and the policy of the administration were clearly demonstrated. This state was Louisiana. Under the banner of sound currency, "the opponents carried everything before them." New Orleans went Whig, as did similar other portions of the state, much to the delight of the "panic" followers. This was the first election Louisiana had participated in since the crisis, and her opposition was recorded in unmistakable terms.[2]

Meanwhile, the same issues were engaging the attention of the voters in the West. Party lines in Illinois were distinctly drawn, and the issues of Sub-treasury and no Sub-treasury were prominent. The main issue in the campaign was internal improvements. The Whigs did not oppose internal improvements, but their candidate advocated the building of railroads with private capital, instead of state aid for canals. Nevertheless, members in Congress were held responsible for the way they had voted on

[1] Letcher to Van Buren, April 28, May 12, 1838, Van Buren MSS. Cf. also Ambler, *Ritchie*, p. 204; Ambler, *Sectionalism in Virginia, 1776–1851*, pp. 229, 230.

[2] *Albany Argus*, July 23, 1838.

the Sub-treasury, and the Whigs worked hard to unseat the supporters of the bill. But their efforts were unavailing, and though the Whigs made some gains in particular counties, they lost the election.[1] The same state of affairs existed in Ohio. Due to the difficulty caused by the Mahan extradition case, which led some to think the Whigs and Abolitionists were working together, due to the lessening of the financial pressure, and due to the efficient work of Senator Allen, the Democrats carried the state, and Wilson Shannon was elected governor.[2] But in the neighboring state of Indiana, the Whigs secured a majority in the assembly.[3]

Thus at the close of the elections of 1838, the political aspect presented a different appearance from that of the previous year. The Democrats had carried Ohio, Maine, Illinois, Alabama, Missouri, Maryland, New Jersey, Pennsylvania, and South Carolina. Their rivals succeeded in carrying New York, Massachusetts, New Hampshire, Connecticut, Rhode Island, Mississippi, North Carolina, Virginia, Georgia, Louisiana, and Indiana. The total number of states in the Whig ranks still outnumbered the administration party, but the results

---

[1] Moses, *Illinois*, I, 425; Thompson, *The Illinois Whigs before 1841*, pp. 59, 60.

[2] Dawson to Jackson, August 28, 1838, Jackson MSS; *Globe*, November 15, 1838.

[3] Niles, August 25, 1838.

failed to satisfy the Whig leaders. Biddle confessed
that the elections had not gone as anticipated,
and laid the blame to the distractions of the Whigs,
rather than to the strength of their adversaries. But
the Democrats accredited their success to the lessening of the money pressure.[1] And perhaps this explanation best accounts for the political reversals.
The readjustment of the money market deprived
the Whigs of their most effective weapon, and as the
demands of labor grew less insistent, the fears of
Locofocoism declined. Only the Sub-treasury remained omnipresent, and on this point the Democrats had the aid of Calhoun, thus assuring support
in the South. Twice the government and the banks
had appealed to the people, and twice they had
received an inconclusive answer. Yet a definite
result had to be rendered, for Congress was still
occupied with this question, and so once more the
parties prepared for another offensive.

The elections of 1839 were even less hopeful in
some respects than those of 1838 for the Whigs. The
Democrats carried Maine, New Hampshire, Massachusetts, Pennsylvania, Maryland, North Carolina, Indiana, Georgia, Tennessee, while the Whigs
carried Vermont, Connecticut, Rhode Island, New
York, New Jersey, Virginia, and Michigan. Their
greatest support came in New York, where,

[1] Biddle to Poinsett, July 11, 1838, B.P.; *Albany Argus*,
August 25, 1838.

once more, the small-bill issue played into their hands.[1] But their most severe setback came in Indiana and Tennessee. The latter result was explained by the excellent campaign of Polk, as against the slow, prosaic methods of his opponent, Newton Cannon.[2] But the overwhelming defeat in Indiana caused the Whigs much anxiety. Another year, and Van Buren might wipe out the terrible defeats of 1837. But before this took place, the nation was to go through the agonies of the crisis of 1839, the final struggle in Congress to pass the Sub-treasury bill, and the preparations for the exciting campaign of 1840. The defeat of the Sub-treasury in 1838 allayed the interests of the people; the nation thought that the struggle had been fought out in Congress. Biddle and his associates were confident that they had succeeded. Enthusiasm abated, and those who were discontented awaited the coming presidential election to express their wishes, rather than trust to state or congressional contests.

The elections of 1839 helped awaken the Whigs to the necessity of conducting a vigorous campaign in 1840. They realized that in each state local issues had helped determine the result, but the psychological effect upon the party situation by the

[1] Marcy to Wetmore, November 7, 1839, Marcy MSS.

[2] *Globe*, August 21, 22, 1839; *Nat. Intell.*, August 12, 19, 1839; cf. also McCormac, *J. K. Polk*, pp. 150, 151.

loss of certain states was the same whether due to national or local problems. Then a direct appeal was made in 1840, not alone to the emotional desires of the electorate, especially in the West, for a change of administration, but also to their pecuniary interests. The unwise statements of Buchanan and Walker that wages were too high in this country, and that it was the intention of the administration to reduce the price of labor, played into the hands of the Whigs.[1] The *Cincinnati Daily Gazette* pointed out that laborers on the Baltimore and Ohio were receiving $62\frac{1}{2}$ cents a day in 1840, as against $1.25 when they commenced work on the road. "Throw up your caps, hard money boys," exclaimed the writer, "and hurrah for Van Buren and low wages. Sixty-two cents a day with a wife and two or three children to feed and clothe. . . . . But that is more than a Cuban negro's labors are considered worth, and the Cuba-negro standard Senator Walker has set up as the one which should prevail. There must be a still further reduction, boys, of from twenty to thirty cents." Moreover, while laborers at Wheeling were receiving $125 per year, Van Buren, "who claims to be the poor man's friend, receives $25,000 a year, lives in a splendid palace supplied and furnished at the nation's

[1] Cf. Walker's statements in *Cong. Globe, Twenty-sixth Cong., First Sess.,* App., p. 142; for Buchanan, cf. *Cincinnati Daily Gazette,* March 9, 1840.

expense, and rides in an English coach accompanied by liveried outriders and drawn by six blooded horses."

A similar appeal was made to the farmer vote in 1840. With farm products selling at one-third less than the figure of 1836, the appeal of the Whigs fell upon fruitful soil. The *Cincinnati Daily Gazette* wrote succinctly:

In 1836 a farmer brought 100 bushels of wheat to market. He got for it $125 cash. He bought 100 pounds of coffee at 14 cents, $14.00; 10 pounds of tea at 75 cents, $7.50; 10 yards of cassimere at $1.50, $15.00; 8 yards of calico at $1.00, $8.00; one bridle, $2.00; and one pound of cavendish tobacco, $37\frac{1}{2}$ cents. He then had $85.12\frac{1}{2}$ to carry home. He goes to market in June, 1840, with his 100 bushels of wheat; sells it, and buys the same articles. What does he now carry home? Twelve and a half cents! Is not the farmer the loser of $85 by the present state of things?[1]

Little wonder that with such propaganda, aided by the slogans, songs, and picnics of 1840, together with the general restlessness of the people, the Whigs swept the nation in 1840! The election of 1840 was the natural consequence of the panic of 1837.

For three years Van Buren went before the people on the issues initiated by the crisis of 1837. In state and congressional elections the Sub-treasury was the point of departure. It disrupted the Democratic party; it helped fan the labor troubles, bring-

[1] *Cincinnati Daily Gazette*, March 5, August 3, 1840.

ing into prominence the Locofoco doctrines; it aided Calhoun to return to the administration ranks; it tended for a while to weaken the Democratic hold on the farmers of the country; it allowed the third parties—Locofocos in New York, and the Democratic Conservatives—to exercise an influence on political matters altogether out of proportion; it brought Van Buren in direct conflict with Biddle, as had been Jackson; it raised definitely the relation of state and bank in the United States; and it prepared the way for the Whig victory in 1840. But the elections did not decide the question. As the panic lost its sting, the Whigs lost their rallying cry. As long as apathy reigned within the Democratic ranks due to the panic and its measures, the Whigs succeeded; but the elections of 1838 showed indications of a counter-reformation in public sentiment. Nothing as yet was decided. Only in Congress, where the fight had been carried on during these years, did the representatives of the sections close the trouble. There, at last, Van Buren was to succeed in checking the United States Bank, close his long contest with Nicholas Biddle, and settle the relations of state and bank in favor of the former.

CHAPTER VI

THE UNITED STATES BANK AND THE RESUMPTION OF SPECIE PAYMENT

In May of 1837 the banks of the United States suspended specie payment, and the country found itself in the throes of the disastrous panic of that year. For seven long weary years the nation was convulsed by an acrimonious debate over the question of a speedy resumption, and during that period all the sectional interests and sectional jealousies, as well as the spirit of division, opposition, selfishness, and cupidity of the banking power of the land were displayed in manifold form. To Nicholas Biddle, the panic afforded an excellent opportunity for securing his former prestige in the financial world. To the administration, it meant the revival of the old conflict between the national government and the United States Bank; while to the deposit banks and to the public at large it was a struggle for existence and security. As the contest progressed, the rivalry between New York and Philadelphia for financial supremacy, and the desire of Nicholas Biddle to protect the credit of his bank and of the nation became self-evident, as a recital of the events of these years discloses.

By April of 1837 the country began to feel the effects of its speculative mania, and the result of Jackson's interference with the financial affairs of the land. As the inevitable collapse of the industrial structure grew apparent, Biddle saw the possibility of once more regaining his lost position. He wrote to Joel R. Poinsett, secretary of war, inclosing a letter from a friend describing the melancholy state of affairs in the West. The reply of the secretary opened the way for a *rapprochement.* "Can you not," wrote Poinsett on May 6, 1837, "in your financial knowledge and experience devise some plan by which a wholesome control may be exercised over bank issues, and bank exchanges be brought back to what they were before the destruction of the Bank—a measure apart from a national bank, even though it might be connected with the operations of a great state institution."[1] The letter was answered with avidity, intimating that "the best thing which Mr. Van Buren could do in reference to himself personally, as well as to his political party, would be to make peace with the Bank." Fearing that this suggestion might not be presented in the most forceful manner, Biddle himself made a trip to Washington to see the President, while agents of the Bank approached the administration through its friends.[2]

[1] McGrane, *Correspondence of Nicholas Biddle*, p. 273.

[2] *Ibid.*, pp. 274–77; for Biddle's trips to Washington, cf. Kane to Van Buren, May 20, 1837, Van Buren MSS.

But while the "Little Magician" hesitated, the storm descended on the land. Within a week suspensions were general throughout the country. Nicholas Biddle had failed to avert the crisis. He now determined to make no moves for resumption until he saw definitely what the new administration intended to do.

It was just two days after the Philadelphia bank suspended that Nicholas Biddle, in an open letter to J. Q. Adams, attempted to justify the actions of his own bank, while at the same time outlining a general policy for the banks to pursue during the interim. The United States Bank had suspended, claimed the writer, in order to protect its own funds in view of the general suspension. Henceforth its efforts would be directed toward keeping itself strong and toward making itself stronger, for the bank must be "always prepared and always anxious to assist" in re-establishing the currency. It would co-operate cordially and zealously with the government, with the government banks, and with all other influences which could aid in that object. In the meantime, however, two great necessities devolved on the banks of the country. The first was to pay to the "utmost farthing" our debts to foreign creditors; the second was to render the suspension as short as possible, "waiting patiently and calmly for the action of the government." Simply put, the banks were to adopt a "watchful waiting policy" until the government revealed its attitude. If the present administration assumed a more conciliatory and understanding appreciation of financial problems than its predecessor, the period of uncertainty and confusion would soon pass; if not, the responsibility for its continuance rested on the shoulders of the government, and not on those of the banks. Any movement, therefore, on the part of the banks looking to resumption would be premature, and might be injurious until they knew what action the Congress would take. If the banks attempted to resume at once, they would have to suspend again, which would only make the matter worse. Then again, if they resumed now, while the government did not change its course, how could they explain why they suspended at all? "By undertaking anything" they acknowledged that they had done wrong, thereby "removing the responsibility from the government."[1]

Throughout the months of May and June no intimations came as to the plans of the administration. By July, Biddle realized, however, that Van Buren did not intend to depart, if possible, from the course of his predecessor.[2] With the earliest intimation of continued hostility upon the part of the government toward the banks, the amnesty came to an end. The parleys were over, and from July,

[1] *National Gazette*, May 16, 1837.
[2] Biddle to Rathbone, July 14, 1837, B.P.

1837, Biddle set to work preparing for the coming struggle.

As might be expected, the obvious move was to strengthen his own institution. In 1836 the United States Bank had negotiated two loans abroad; and in March, 1837, it had contracted heavy additional liabilities, upon the application of the merchants of New York, by issuing bonds payable in London. The question was how to provide means for paying off this indebtedness. One possible method was to enter the cotton market, where, owing to the derangement of the currency, the staple of the South was selling at a low figure. In the first place, the Bank could get the advantage of a large circulation of its notes; it would get the premium of its drafts from the South; it would get the funds of Europe without the least danger, and a large collection of its southern debts. More important still, the possession of these funds abroad would be the means of protecting and saving the Bank from prostration. Furthermore, the operation would be of great advantage to the whole country. By introducing a new competitor into the market, the unconditional subjection of the planter to the foreign purchaser might be prevented. The latter would be compelled to give something like its real value for the southern staple. In haughty disregard of the public clamor which he realized would be aroused by such actions, the audacious financier embarked on this

campaign during the summer months. The Bank
established an agency in London under the management of Samuel Jaudon, the Bank's cashier,
while a new commission house of Humphreys and
Biddle appeared in London to handle the cotton
shipments.[1]

According to Humphreys, the arrival of Jaudon
was viewed with alarm by the "old women of
Threadneedle Street,"who were filled with an uncon-
querable jealousy toward the growing commerce of
America and its grand "moneyed machine." The
merchants and manufacturers of England, however, welcomed any means that would supply the
cotton needs for their factories. Notwithstanding
the numerous failures of crippled concerns, there
seemed to be a great abundance of capital at the
disposal of the sound houses, and, combined with
the moderate stock of cotton then in the country,
there soon developed a good field for operations.[2]

[1] Biddle explained his cotton transactions in detail in a letter
to John M. Clayton, published in *National Gazette*, April 10, 1841;
cf. also Biddle to Roberts, July 31, August 9, September 15, 1837,
in *P.L.B.* Biddle's son Edward was a partner in the commission
house of Humphreys and Biddle. The foreign loans mentioned
above were negotiated by Samuel Jaudon—one of £1,000,000, in
London, to be repaid in four equal instalments, two in 1837, and
two in 1838; the other in Paris, of 12,500,000 francs, payable in six
equal instalments, two of which were to be paid in each of the years
1837, 1838, and 1839.

[2] Humphreys to Biddle, November 23, 1837, B.P. There are
numerous letters of Humphreys to Biddle expressing the same con-
victions as this one.

By December, 1837, the Liverpool papers were commending the energetic and wise measures of the United States Bank in contributing to the return of confidence, as Americans began to discharge their obligations.[1] But long before this, Biddle had turned his attention to another phase of the contest.

This was nothing more than the solidifying of the banking power of the land in the protection of their rights against any further assaults of the government. In attempting this, Biddle began to appreciate the sectional interest and local jealousies within financial circles. Jackson's ferocious attack on the United States Bank had disrupted the whole fabric of the business world, and the results of his handiwork now revealed themselves. The ancient animosity of the state banks toward the monster of Pennsylvania, the desire of the deposit banks to remove from their own shoulders the odium of bringing on the suspension, and the secret hope of Nicholas Biddle to reassume his old position began to clash.

The banks of Philadelphia had received an appeal from those of New York, eight days after the suspension, to meet in convention in New York "for the purpose of agreeing on a time when specie payments should be resumed, and on the measures to

[1] Newspaper clipping, marked Liverpool, December 30, 1837, in B.P., and underlined.

effect that purpose." The reason assigned for the invitation was "that it would be impracticable for those of any particular section to resume without a general explanation of at least the principal banks of the great parts of the country." Suspecting the declaration was but a move on the part of the deposit banks to show their penitence, with the hope that they might be trusted again, the banks of Philadelphia, at the instigation of Biddle, refused the request on August 29. Baltimore and Boston followed Philadelphia in stating their belief that the general resumption of specie payment depended "mainly, if not exclusively, on the action of Congress"; and without the latter's co-operation, "all attempts at a general system of payments in coin . . . . must be partial and temporary." Chagrined by this rebuff, the New York banks were forced to await the assembling of Congress.[1]

The President offered them little consolation. In his message to Congress, Van Buren suggested the designation of certain public offices to keep and disburse the public money. Intimate friends of Biddle stated that the United States Bank would have to act as a mediator between the government

[1] *National Gazette*, April 10, 1838. This account summarizes Philadelphia's attitude on resumption up to 1838. For Biddle's reactions to the request, and the pressure he brought to bear on Boston and Buffalo, cf. Biddle to Rathbone, July 11, 1837; to Abbott Lawrence, August 30, 1837; to James Hamilton, August 30, 1837, B.P. Also Adams, J. Q., *Memoirs*, IX, 364.

and the deposit banks.[1] The administration had played directly into the hands of its opponents. The deposit banks had been first cajoled, then nearly ruined, then insulted, and now deserted. When a second invitation came, therefore, from the New York banks, on October 21, for a similar meeting on November 27, Philadelphia, "not wanting to appear discourteous," decided to send delegates.[2]

For six days the convention was in session behind closed doors, but Biddle was kept closely informed of its proceedings by his friends. The New York banks were anxious for a speedy resumption, since they were required by law to resume by May 16, 1838. The Philadelphia banks were determined to leave the decision upon the subject to a future meeting. A committee of one delegate from each state was appointed to report on resumption. During the debate, the discordant elements in the banking forces became evident. The country banks of New York asserted that if the city banks of New York would not unite with them, and the convention should adjourn without fixing a date, they would resume themselves. Then if the city banks did not pay their balances to the country banks, they would sue the former. Rumors were circulated that the Philadelphia banks threatened the New York banks with annihilation if they attempted resumption on

[1] Biddle to Davis, September 7, 1837, B.P.

[2] *National Gazette*, April 10, 1838.

their own accord.[1] As the discussion progressed, the
jealousies and hostilities against the United States
Bank and the local feeling against the whole state of
Pennsylvania and her improvements became apparent. As one correspondent wrote Biddle, the feeling
was strong "that Pennsylvania must have her
wings clipped, and New York must take the ascendency in internal improvements and moneyed operations."[2] But the Pennsylvania men were too
strongly intrenched to be overcome. A friend of
the United States Bank had been selected as chairman; the New England delegates, especially Boston,
worked in close harmony with Pennsylvania; the
committee could not agree on a report; and the
advantageous arrival of the long-desired delegate
from Delaware strengthened the ranks of those
opposed to resumption.[3] The majority of the committee agreed on July 1 as the proper time for resumption; while the minority reported that in the
opinion of the convention, "the present circumstances of the country are not such to make it
expedient or prudent now to fix a day for resuming."
The vote was taken by states, and the majority

[1] Throop to Van Buren, November 29, 1837, Van Buren MSS.
New York Law, in *Laws of New York*, (1837) pp. 515–17.

[2] Eyre to Biddle, November 28, 1837, B.P. Cf. also, Adams,
Memoirs, IX, 445, 446.

[3] Eyre to Biddle, November 29, 1837, B.P.; Throop to Van
Buren, November 30, 1837; Edmonds to Van Buren, December 2,
1837, Van Buren MSS.

report was defeated on a count of eleven to seven.[1] As Edmonds wrote Van Buren, the officers had been chosen from other states, and "New York, who called the convention, and was most deeply interested in the result, had no more voice than Indiana, and the presidents and cashiers of New York, who by their proceeding had been appointed at least lookers on, were turned out of the doors *sans* ceremony, and the seven were left 'alone in their glory.'"[2] Pennsylvania had carried the day; but the obstinacy of New York was most threatening, as Biddle and his associates fully realized. On December 3 the convention adjourned to meet on April 11 for the purpose "of considering, and, if practical, determining upon a day when the payments might be resumed."

New York had not given up all hope, however, of persuading Philadelphia of the unwisdom of her proceeding. On January 7, one of the leading New York bankers wrote Biddle that the reputation and future usefulness of the banking power rested upon resumption within ninety days. Unless they resumed within that period, confidence would swing

[1] Those in favor of striking out the majority report were Pennsylvania, Vermont, New Hampshire, Massachusetts, Rhode Island, Connecticut, New Jersey, Maryland, South Carolina, Indiana, Delaware. Those opposed were New York, Virginia, Ohio, Georgia, North Carolina, Kentucky, and the District of Columbia. Cf. *New York Journal of Commerce*, December 6, 1837.

[2] Edmonds to Van Buren, December 2, 1837, Van Buren MSS.

from its moorings, and all faith in their integrity, as well as in their ability, would be lost. It was useless, moreover, to hope for a national bank. The nation would never permit the present Bank of the United States to become a national institution. Whenever the country is ripe for such a bank, "a new one will undoubtedly be created." It was, therefore, to the interest of Pennsylvania that the credit of the state institutions should be preserved, since her own, powerful as the Bank might be, could never hope to survive the downfall of those of her sister states. Furthermore, the resumption of specie payment was as essential from the political as it was from the fiscal point of view. "It would take away the necessity, or rather the pretext, for a Sub-treasury, and tumble their [the Democrats'] political scaffolding to the ground."

The writer then exhorted Biddle to exert his power, assume the "fiscal scepter," and rule this "fierce democracy of banks as Charlemagne ruled the once formidable but disjointed empire of the Caesars"; show the banks that his and their interests were identical, as all were alike free from any entangling alliance with the government. New York must resume, since her laws required it; but her merchants were not unaware of the peril she would encounter if she stood forth as the only specie-paying city in the union. If it were known that the Bank of the United States had determined to do likewise, "confidence would be restored, business would revive, and even the political horizon would lighten up."[1]

The appeal, nevertheless, went unheeded. So long as the government upheld the enforcement of the Specie Circular, which forbade the receipt of anything but gold and silver at the land offices; so long as the administration pressed forward its plans for a Sub-treasury; and so long as the Legislature of Pennsylvania did not fix a time for resumption, there was no need to be "rushed into resumption" merely to satisfy New York.[2] Any premature action would place the United States Bank at the mercy of

[1] Worth to Biddle, January 7, 1838, B.P. Biddle replied, on January 20, in the following strain: "You do me but justice in ascribing to me a strong disposition to aid . . . . although you overrate greatly my power to be useful. That power, such as it is, will be gladly used in any form which promises to be beneficial." On the twenty-first Worth wrote again, reiterating his old argument and assuring Biddle that the New York City banks were anxious to establish a good understanding with the Philadelphia banks, and with the United States Bank in particular. "The past, therefore," wrote Worth, "whatever it may have been, ought not to interfere with the present. It is not, I think, characteristic of clever men to be turned aside from any great or important object by personal feeling or personal resentment. . . . . I know you are above and beyond them." No reply was necessary to this letter, as Biddle had set forth his ideas in that of the twentieth instant.

[2] When the Bank of the United States was chartered by Pennsylvania, Biddle had been careful to see that it did not allow the legislature to alter or repeal the charter at pleasure. Thus the legislature could not touch the Bank for non-payment of specie. At a later date (1841) this same question of forfeiture of charter

the government. If the latter threw treasury notes on the market after the Bank had agreed to make its payment in specie, the Bank's own depositors would exhaust the supply of gold and silver in its vaults in purchasing these notes. It was much wiser, therefore, to remain on the defensive. "The credit system and the specie systems were now face to face—one or the other must fall."[1] Those who were charged with the preservation of the credit system, which had built up the country, must make no sortie lest they be cut off, nor leave their intrenchments until they saw the enemy retreating. For these reasons, on January 31, the Philadelphia banks, in reply to an inquiry from New York concerning the naming of a day, refused to comply favorably with the request, on the ground that it would be disrespectful to take any steps until the bank convention reassembled in April.[2]

The force of circumstances impelled the New York banks to make further efforts toward resumption even in the light of this second rebuke. The public was clamoring for resumption, and by statute

---

for non-payment of specie was decided in favor of the Bank. Cf. Biddle's letter to Clayton, quoted in *National Gazette*, April 12, 1841. Pennsylvania was not being rushed into resumption in 1838 because Biddle was in close touch with the legislature, and through the aid of his lieutenant, F. Fraley, had killed all such moves. Cf. Biddle to Fraley, March 4, 8, 21, 1838, in *P.L.B.*

[1] Biddle to Gamble, January 31, 1838, *P.L.B.*

[2] *National Gazette*, April 10, 1838.

the banks would lose their charters if they failed to act on or before May 16. By January 1, 1838, the city banks of New York, exclusive of the Dry Dock Bank, had diminished their liabilities more than $12,500,000, while the balance of more than $4,000,-000 was due them by banks outside of the state, and of more than $2,000,000 in account with all the banks outside the city. Moreover, the country bank statements disclosed the fact that they could redeem their notes which circulated in the city; while the fall in the rate of foreign exchange, "now considerably below par in New York City paper," rendered it absolutely certain that no exportation of specie could take place. Determined, therefore, to force the issue, the leading bankers of New York City met in convention and determined to resume by May 10, hoping that at the last moment Biddle and the Philadelphia bankers would co-operate with them.[1]

Biddle, however, remained adamant, meanwhile devoting his attention to the crushing of the Sub-treasury bill then being debated in the Senate. The Senate passed the bill, however, on March 26, by a vote of 27 to 25.[2] This reaction, coming as it

[1] *Ibid.*, March 3, 1838. The meeting took place February 28. The above statistics are based on the bank commissioner's report, as used by this convention. *Summary of Commissioner's Report*, Niles, February 10, 1838.

[2] Cf. next chapter for this struggle in the Senate.

did just as New York was moving toward resumption, boded ill for the plans of the Philadelphia financier. In various sections he was being blamed for the continued suspension; and even his friends in New England were beginning to show signs of weakness. Some drastic action was necessary to hearten the banking forces in their fight on the administration; and the most effective mode of accomplishing this would be a complete statement of Philadelphia's position.

On April 5, 1838, Biddle issued this explanation in a letter to John Quincy Adams. The question before the nation was whether, after all, the time had arrived when the banks should announce that the causes of suspension had ceased to exist, and that the suspension need no longer be continued. If one examined the situation, however, he would find that none of these causes had ceased to exist. The Specie Circular was not repealed. On the contrary, it had been extended, for bank notes were proscribed not merely for the land offices, but for all payments of every description to the government. True, the distribution of the surplus was over, because there was no longer any surplus to distribute, but the hostility engendered by the propaganda of the government against bank notes had created an implacable hostility toward these instruments of credit. Thus the credit system and the metallic system were now fairly in the field. "One or the other must fall. There could be no other issue. The present struggle must be final." If the banks resumed, and by sacrificing the community continued to sustain themselves for a few months, it would be "conclusively employed at the next elections to show that the schemes of the executive were not as destructive as they will prove hereafter. But if they resume and again are compelled to suspend, the executive will rejoice at his new triumph, and they will fall in the midst of a universal outcry against their weakness." By public clamor the banks were being driven toward a political and forced resumption, rather than a business resumption.

Perceiving nothing in the conduct of the government to justify an early resumption, the writer then turned to an analysis of the condition of the nation's affairs. The suspension had found the country heavily in debt—not less than $500,000,-000, with large balances from southern and western states to the Atlantic states—and owing a considerable debt to Europe. The disease of the country had been brought on by an overstrained and distempered energy. The remedy needed was repose. With this in mind, the United States Bank since suspension had diminished its loans less than 10 per cent, while, by aiding in the moving of the crops of the South to the markets, it had saved the planting interests "probably from ten to fifteen millions

of dollars," and had added to the Bank's specie
$3,000,000.

But it might be said that the credit of the country would be injured by not resuming. "Not in the
least," asserted Biddle. "What Europeans want
now is that we should pay our debts . . . . and if
they [the Europeans] see, as they cannot fail to see,
that these premature efforts will prevent the collection of what is due them, they will understand that
in endeavoring to secure an object wholly domestic
they have been sacrificed."

Moreover, the month of May was a bad time to
resume, because the resumption, to be useful, must
be general, and no arrangement could be satisfactory which did not include the South and West.
These were not yet ready to resume, and the crop
movements at this time of the year did not aid
them. For example, it took fifty days to take cotton
from New Orleans to Liverpool. Supposing it was
immediately sold, the usage was to give, at the end
of ten days, a banker's acceptance payable in two
months, so that by May there would not be actually realized more than the cotton which left New
Orleans before January, when not more than a
fourth or a fifth of the whole crop had been shipped.
Furthermore, spring was the season when the credits for the shipments of the southern and western
produce were maturing at the north; when the
western business had brought from the interior

the notes of the Atlantic banks; when the circulation pressed more upon them than at any other period; and when specie was needed for the trade to China and India.

The course the Bank should adopt was, therefore, simply this: a *status quo* should be maintained —preparing to resume, but not resuming. They should begin by paying the small notes, so as to restore coin to all the minor channels of circulation; but they should make no general resumption until they ascertained what course the government would pursue, "employing, in the meantime, their whole power to forward the crops to market." "The Americans should," concluded Biddle, do, in short, what the American Army did at New Orleans, "stand fast behind their cotton bales until the enemy had left the country."[1] As the New York banks seemed unwilling to do this, Philadelphia resolved not to attend the coming bank convention in April.[2]

[1] *National Gazette*, April 7, 10, 1838. The cotton trade of these years was as follows (M. B. Hammond, *The Cotton Industry*, 1897):

Year	Total Exports of U.S. in Thousands of Bales	Total Exports of U.S. to Great Britain, in Thousands of Bales	Average New York Prices for Middling Upland, in Cents	Average Liverpool Prices for Middling Upland, in Cents
1837..........	1,168	851	82.05	6.09
1838..........	1,576	1,165	67.83	6.28
1839..........	1,075	798	79.18	7.19

[2] *National Gazette*, April 10, 1838.

By his friends, Biddle's letter was considered a master-stroke; by his enemies it was heralded as a *faux pas*. "Our friends had become nervous, and stood in need of something to invigorate them. This will have the effect," wrote Sergeant to Biddle.[1] At the same time, Van Buren was assured that Biddle had committed a grievous blunder.[2] He had written as a dictator, and had attempted to array all the banks against the government. In haughty disdain of the public clamor for resumption, he had commanded all the banks to "prepare to resume, but not to resume." But some of the state institutions were not entirely certain that the administration was unfriendly toward them. If the opportunity were seized of opposing the resuming institutions against the non-resuming—for example, the New York banks against the Philadelphia banks—the strength of the money power would be weakened, and time would be given the people to rally to the aid of the government. By assisting and cheering these banks to throw off the thraldom of the Philadelphia autocrat, happy and important consequences might ensue.[3] A coup d'état was possible, but haste was necessary. So urged Van Buren's friends. Just as these suggestions reached the President, and the adjourned bank convention

[1] Sergeant to Biddle, April 9, 1838, B.P.

[2] Throop to Van Buren, April 9, 1838, Van Buren MSS.

[3] Parker to Van Buren, April 10, 1838, Van Buren MSS.

reassembled in New York, a resolution was presented in the House which seemed to indicate that the plan had been adopted.

On April 7, Hamer of Ohio submitted for consideration a resolution to the effect that if the banks, or a portion of them, resumed, it should be the duty of the general government, "within the limits of its constitutional authority, to aid such banks . . . . in regaining public confidence, and to sustain them in their laudable efforts." As the author was known to be a leader of the administration forces, his action immediately attracted attention.[1] Was the government, as Webster thought, about to abandon the Sub-treasury, and was this the first advance toward the banks?[2] Or had it been offered merely as a counter proposition to Biddle's letter, with the design of dividing the bank forces into two distinct groups? Various opinions were expressed concerning its real intent as the delegates to the bank convention began to meet in New York; and interest increased as Hamer was refused permission to explain his resolution, and rumor spread that Washington and Albany had been appealed to by the New Yorkers. The latter was quite true, for early

[1] The full story of Hamer's resolution is given in the *Congressional Globe, Twenty-fifth Cong., Second Sess.*, pp. 288, 297, 307, 309, 311. J. Q. Adams in his *Memoirs*, IX, 375, described Hamer as "sly as a Quaker, and as sour as a Presbyterian."

[2] Webster to Biddle, April 9, 1838, B.P.

in March, Gallatin had approached Flagg on this subject,[1] and one day, after the convention began its work, Governor Marcy sent a special message[2] to the legislature, proposing the issuance of state stock "for the enlargement of the Erie Canal and the completion of the Black River and Genesee Valley canals," to the amount of six or eight million dollars which could be loaned to the banks in case of an emergency; while on March 18, Woodbury privately assured the banks of New York of the settled policy of the department to promote the resumption of specie payment.[3] But Biddle's letter and the non-attendance of the Philadelphia delegates strengthened the hands of the non-resumers. Something more specific than Hamer's resolution was necessary to hearten the efforts of New York.

This was furnished from three sources. On the thirteenth an open letter from Woodbury was read to the convention, in which he stated that the government would continue to receive the bills of

[1] Gallatin to Flagg, March 6, 1838, Flagg MSS.

[2] Flagg to Van Buren, April 12, 1838, Van Buren MSS; cf. also Ward to Marcy, March 20, 1838, Marcy MSS; Marcy message in Niles, April 28, 1838.

[3] Printed in *National Gazette*, April 11, 1838. Biddle had tried to find out if the New York Legislature could not be induced to prolong the period of suspension, and had been assured of the impossibility of such a contingency (Biddle to Ogden, April 4, 1838, and reply of Ogden to Biddle, April 10, B.P.). The nervousness and lack of unity in the New York banking circles is clearly demonstrated in Blatchford to Biddle, March 26, 27, 1838, B.P.

specie-paying banks when at par where offered, and
that such bills would be paid whenever they were
acceptable to public creditors.[1] Three days later
Grundy declared that the destruction of all banks
was not sought for or desired; that they should be
honest, and obey the laws of the country, and comply with their engagements was anxiously wished
for—nothing more.[2] On the same day Hamer with-
drew his resolution, on the ground that it was un-
necessary in light of the statements of Woodbury
and the comments in the *Globe;* while as a fitting
climax, word came that the Bank of England was
willing to export £1,000,000 to the New York banks
to aid in resumption.[3] In the midst of this sur-
charged atmosphere the convention adjourned, "recommending to all the banks of the several states to
resume specie payments on the first Monday in
January next, without precluding an earlier resumption on the part of such banks as may find it necessary or deem it proper." The delegates from the
state of New York held a meeting immediately

[1] Published in *National Gazette*, April 17, 1838.

[2] *Globe*, April 24, 1838.

[3] The actions of the Bank of England in 1838 are related in
detail in *House of Commons Report of Committee on Banks of Issue*
(1840), pp. 117, 155. There is a significant letter in the Van Buren
MSS (Macaulay to Van Buren, April 20, 1838) relating the pressure brought to bear on the Bank of England to take this action.
The letter also shows that Van Buren was cognizant of the whole
transaction. Cf. also Colt to Biddle, April 16, 1838, B.P.

after the convention closed and agreed to resume on or before May 10.[1]

Even in the face of this disaffection, the United States Bank remained steadfast. The government must be compelled to discontinue its distinction between specie and paper before Biddle would move. This could only be achieved by the withdrawal of the Specie Circular. To this end the friends of the Bank turned their efforts with the result that on May 30 the Specie Circular was repealed in the Senate by a vote of 34 to 9, and in the House by 154 to 29.[2] Realizing that a partial success had been gained, the banker addressed another letter to John Quincy Adams, signifying his willingness to "co-operate cordially with the government" in promoting an early resumption.[3] With the President's ordinance repealed, the appointment of Woodbury as chief justice of New Hampshire, which amounted to a dismissal, and a request from New York to establish a branch bank there, it looked as if a civil revolution had taken place on the side of the Bank. "I shall not be very much surprised," wrote Biddle to Jaudon, "if some coquetting passes between our administration friends

---

[1] *New York Journal of Commerce*, April 17, 1838.

[2] For Webster's account of the origin of the motion to repeal the Specie Circular, cf. McGrane, *op. cit.*, pp. 310, 311.

[3] *New York Journal of Commerce*, June 6, 1838; *National Gazette*, May 31, 1838.

and the Bank, as we are in a singularly amiable mood."[1]

Nevertheless the fight was not over. The House still had to decide the fate of the Sub-treasury bill. Accordingly, the Philadelphia banks determined not to move until after Congress adjourned, and then, "having collected the views of the distant banks," to invite those of Boston, Baltimore, and Richmond to a meeting in which some general day of resumption would be named. On June 25 the House negatived the Sub-treasury bill by 125 to 111, and on July 9 Congress adjourned. Four days later Governor Ritner issued a proclamation calling upon the banks to resume by August 13, and on July 23 a bank convention met in Philadelphia, composed of delegates from Massachusetts, Rhode Island, Delaware, Virginia, Connecticut, Pennsylvania, Maryland, and Kentucky, at which the date fixed by the governor was agreed to by all present.[2]

Meanwhile the transaction, the strangest in all this long contest between Bank and government, had taken place. On July 11, Mr. Kimball, of the House of Representatives, on behalf of the secretary of war, called upon Biddle to know whether the bonds of the Bank given as security for the debt due to the government at the expiration of the charter as a national bank could be made available "for the

[1] McGrane, op. cit., p. 312.

[2] National Gazette, July 13, 24, 25, 1838.

use of the department." Seizing the chance, Biddle agreed to advance the money needed on the first, second, and perhaps third, bonds, "if it could be made to the interest of both the department and the Bank." Therefore, if the secretary would arrange to have the bonds placed at his disposal to raise the money on them, and let the United States Bank of Pennsylvania know "how, where, and when" the disbursements were to be made, "the Bank would be glad to lend its aid." Thus the Bank of the United States, a state institution, was to become once more the depository of the government funds, as Biddle wrote to one of his friends:

After all the nonsense of the last few years the government takes in payment of a bond a credit in a bank which does not yet pay specie, and which has declared that it did not mean to pay specie until that very government had abandoned its course. . . . . We resume on the thirteenth of this month. We begin without having sacrificed any great interest. We begin with a wide circle of resumers whom our delay has enabled to prepare, and begin after having beaten down the government and secured the ascendency of reason for the future. We arrive in port without having been under the necessity of throwing over any of our cargo. We arrive for every useful purpose just as soon as our neighbors who lost overboard a large part of their passengers; and we only stopped on the way to sink a pirate. So that, on the whole, I had no reason to be dissatisfied with our course.[1]

Now that the great contest was over, all the participants claimed the victory. According to the

---

[1] McGrane, *op. cit.*, pp. 318, 321.

Globe, the action of the New York banks had demonstrated that the national bank was not necessary to compel the state banks to resume specie payments, and, furthermore, that a single state could not only successfully resume without resumption in any other state, but against great and violent resistance in other states.[1] In the December message to Congress, Van Buren declared that by the withholding of the fourth instalment of the surplus; the issuance of treasury notes; the refusal to employ as general depositories, or receive the notes of, such banks as declined to redeem their notes in specie, aided by the favorable action of some of the banks, and by the support and co-operation of a large portion of the community, an early resumption had been secured.[2] Woodbury claimed that the treasury, in refusing to accept depreciated paper, and by aiding and abetting, the state banks had achieved the desired end, even though it had been opposed by "many banks as well as by some influential individuals."[3] While Biddle, in a letter on the subject to J. Q. Adams, reiterated that the movement of cotton "had not only secured the planter interests from destruction, but had helped to pay off one-half of the commercial debt of this country to

[1] *Globe*, August 28, 1838.

[2] *Senate Doc., Twenty-fifth Cong., Third Sess.*, Vol. I, No. 1, pp. 13, 14.

[3] *Ibid.*, No. 2, pp. 14–16.

Europe, by the mere difference between the actual
sale of these securities and staples, and the prices the
southerners would have realized had they been
thrown unprotected into the hands of Europeans."[1]
Later investigators claimed that these cotton investments had netted a profit of $1,400,000 on the
transaction,[2] while Humphreys and Biddle reported
by April 1, 1839, a gain of $425,000 for their house.[3]
Lastly, the Bank of England intimated that by
sending its gold to the New York banks it had
materially contributed to the restoration of the
credit. Perhaps no one of these assertions contains
the whole truth, but taken together they do explain
the final outcome.

Wearied with his exertions, Biddle determined
to retire. On March 29, 1839, he resigned the presidency, and the institution was turned over to other
hands. Under the guidance of these men the Bank
started on the last lap of its career, as the country
plunged forward toward a new suspension. The
sudden hope awakened by resumption led many to
believe that all danger was passed. Individuals
started new enterprises; imports began to exceed
exports;[4] the United States Bank continued its

[1] *National Gazette*, December 13, 1838.

[2] Letter of Biddle to Clayton, published in *National Gazette*,
April 10, 1841.

[3] Humphreys to Biddle, May 16, 1839, B.P.

[4] *Senate Doc., Twenty-sixth Cong., First Sess.*, Vol. I, No. 2, p. 3.

policy of cotton advances;[1] and states undertook
vast schemes of internal improvements on loans
often secured from European capitalists eager to aid
a people, who, in the midst of a great calamity, had
shown their willingness to meet their obligations.
The gloom which had spread over the land passed
away, and the nation seemed once more on the
road to recovery.

However, the appearances were deceiving.
"Mere credit had become too commonly the basis
of trade." The banks had become borrowers instead of lenders, and some of them were indulging
in rather dubious proceedings. Among these, the
United States Bank was no exception. By 1839
Humphreys and Biddle had fifty thousand more
bales of cotton than in 1838, which they were holding
under instructions for a rising market, in view of the
diminished crop at home, and the low surplus in the
hands of the manufacturers in England. This action
under ordinary circumstances would have resulted
successfully, but, coming as it did when rumors of
revolutionary prospects in France, political excitement in England between Whigs and Tories, and
the rumblings of the Chartists were unsettling
moneyed conditions, the outlook[2] began to grow

[1] Before Biddle left the presidency he had cautioned his son
concerning the cotton market. It should be noted that Biddle
was now out of office, and cannot be held responsible for what the
Bank did at this period.

[2] Humphreys to Biddle, May 16, July 4, 1839, B.P.

ominous. Moreover, as the demand for yarns and cotton goods on the continent fell off, the English spinners, exasperated at what they thought was the Bank's attempt to monopolize the market, determined to have the residue of the crop at their own figure by working but four days a week;[1] while the Bank of England advanced its rate of interest on bills of exchange and notes to $5\frac{1}{2}$ per cent.[2] Finally, to make matters worse, the harvests of England revealed a shortage in the grain crop. This necessitated a drain of $40,000,000 from the vaults of the Bank of England to purchase grain from neighboring countries, with a corresponding demand upon American debtors to meet their notes. The inevitable outcome was a marked stringency in the banking circles of the United States as specie left America for England.[3] Naturally, the United States Bank, with a surplus of cotton on hand which it could not dispose of in a declining market, and without ready funds to meet its obligations, found

---

[1] *Manchester Guardian*, quoted in *National Intelligencer*, July 29, 1839; cf. also cotton circular in *Philadelphia National Gazette*, July 12, 1839.

[2] *National Intelligencer*, August 21, 1839.

[3] A complete description of the reasons for the panic of 1839, evidently written for publication by Biddle, can be found in the Biddle Papers; while the reasons for the failure of the Philadelphia banks are given in the *National Gazette*, October 25, 1839. On the grain situation, Biddle wrote: "These importations are from the neighboring countries, where grain is cheaper than in England and cheaper than in this country."

itself forced to suspend specie payments on October 9, 1839. The banks of the South and West, also heavily in debt, followed the United States Bank, and by November, 1839, the country was once more in the grip of a panic.

The New England and New York banks, under pressure of their mercantile communities, refused, however, to follow the example of Philadelphia. This called forth much recrimination from the Philadelphia banks. The *National Gazette* justified the Pennsylvania banks, and characterized "the pertinacity with which the New York banks adhered to their resolution to continue specie payments as a kind of fanaticism"; but all to no avail. There was no Biddle to guide the faltering steps of the United States Bank, or coerce the government and the New York banks to submit to Philadelphia's decrees. On all sides the clamor against the banks was resumed as the disclosures of the speculative operations of the "moneyed monster" and its sister institutions were revealed to the public.

With renewed energy Van Buren returned to the assault in the December message of 1839. Recounting the misdeeds of the banks during the past few years, he appealed to American patriotism to free itself from the moneyed power of the United States and England. "To place our foreign and domestic policy under the control of a foreign moneyed interest impaired the independence of our government, as the present credit system has impaired the independence of our banks," proclaimed the President.[1] With unfaltering steadfastness he again proposed to Congress the passage of his favorite measure. The goal was almost in sight.

[1] *Senate Doc., Twenty-fifth Cong., First Sess.*, I, 14–17.

CHAPTER VII

THE STRUGGLE OVER THE INDEPENDENT TREASURY BILL

The interest in the struggle over the Independent Treasury bill—or, as it was popularly known, the Sub-treasury bill—centers around the policy adopted by Nicholas Biddle and the followers of the national bank idea. With the distress attending the panic, the president of the defunct national bank endeavored to get in touch with the administration, hoping to relieve the nation and perhaps benefit his own institution; failing in this, he became the ardent opponent of the measure throughout his career as president of the United States Bank of Pennsylvania. It was not until he had retired, public opinion had expressed itself in several elections, and politics had played into the hands of the Democrats, that the bill became a law. July 4, 1840, closed for the time the long struggle begun by President Jackson.

The suggestion of an independent treasury came to Van Buren from Dr. Brockenbrough of Richmond, Virginia. The doctor proposed a complete divorce of state and bank, and the establishment of a system of federal depositories, two or more to a state, under the charge and management of federal commissioners. Brockenbrough prophesied a clamor would be raised by politicians "about the increased patronage for the appointment of these commissioners, and by the merchants about locking up funds that ought to be profitably used"; but he thought there would not be as much patronage as with the present deposit banks.[1] The idea impressed the President. Immediately Van Buren set about procuring aid for the new scheme. Rives, Tallmadge, Benton, and Wright were informed of the plan, and their advice and aid solicited.[2] Rives soon showed his opposition to the Sub-treasury, advocating instead the retention of "Jackson's selected state banks";[3] while Wright, appreciating the value of the suggestion, declared it could not be carried in Congress. "The Democratic party is already changed by banks," wrote Wright, "and therefore it will not stand for a separation." Moreover, the senator from New York doubted whether it could be enforced after it was carried. Undoubtedly it would prove popular, but not practical.[4] But the President, undeterred by Rives's antagonism and Wright's misgivings, determined to adopt the Sub-

[1] Brockenbrough to Van Buren, May 22, 1837, Van Buren MSS.

[2] Van Buren to Rives, May 25, 1837, Van Buren MSS.

[3] Rives to Van Buren, June 3, 1837, Van Buren MSS.

[4] Wright to Van Buren, June 4, 1837, Van Buren MSS.

treasury as an administration measure, although many of his closest friends doubted the "nerve and moral courage" of the chief executive, fearful that his object in convening Congress was to recharter the United States Bank.[1] Nevertheless, as summer progressed, assurances of hope and success came to the White House from Wright, Flagg, and the Locofocos;[2] and strengthened by these messages Van Buren met the extra session in September, 1837.

When Congress assembled, the President outlined his views, setting forth the main features of the Independent Treasury. In place of a national bank, the President suggested the designation of certain public officers to keep and disburse the public money strictly on a specie basis. The message was received with horror, exultation, and doubt by the various sections of the country. The deposit banks of New York, so Biddle stated, considered themselves the most abused people in the land; and intimate friends of the financier stated that the United States Bank would have to act as a mediator between the government and the deposit banks.[3] "If nothing more is done than is indicated in the message, the Biddle bank party will unmistakably

[1] Mitchell to Polk, June 14, 1837, Polk MSS.

[2] Flagg to ———, July 12, 1837; Riley to Van Buren, July 28, 1837; Wright to Van Buren, June 22, 1837, Van Buren MSS.

[3] Biddle to Davis, September 7, 1837, B.P.

succeed," wrote a friend of Polk. "It is impossible to resist the current . . . . of popular desire to have a regular and uniform paper currency of the same value everywhere. If the present administration does not furnish such a currency, the people will elect men who will do so."[1] "I do not believe the United States Bank can be overcome by a pursuance of the specie policy recommended," reiterated Catron of Tennessee, to Polk:

The old adage that "you must fight the devil with fire" is true very nearly in all party contests, and to the letter in this. Mr. V. B. is presenting a theory sound to the core in principle, but hardly possible in practice; a practice of more than fifty years' standing, based on paper and credit, in our fiscal operations has sapped the public mind and morals, as was intended by its distinguished founder, Mr. Hamilton, to this fearful extent; it has made Federalists of about the entire trading community, and of most of the wealthy of other avocations, and especially of very many of our profession, who are politicians. I mean by Federalists, such as seek to govern by wealth opposed to numbers, or to govern the country by cities and villages. They command the surplus money and the press, and at this time they possess a great accidental advantage, that of financial embarrassment; and they possess another: They set up their claims to power with a bank already in existence, tangible and understood, whose paper was distinguished for its high comparative value during a time far back in the recollection of the present generation of young men. . . . . The opposition declared that the old state of things—commercial credit, sound currency— would in a month be restored by a recharter of the Bank,

[1] Walker to Polk, September 10, 1837, Polk MSS.

which is constantly kept before the public by all the talent and appliances that money can buy. . . . . As well might we undertake to overthrow a mountain with a shadow.[1]

In truth, with the appearance of the Conservatives under the leadership of Tallmadge of New York, and Rives of Virginia, with whom Biddle was already in close touch,[2] the bank men might feel well pleased with the message. Only from Jackson,[3] the Locofocos, and a few intimate and steadfast friends did the President receive any word of encouragement upon the stand he had taken. But the die had been cast, and "seemingly willing to stand in the breach and nobly fall in the attempt," Van Buren awaited the action of Congress.[4]

On September 14, Senator Wright of New York, as chairman of the Committee on Finance, reported the bill to establish an Independent Treasury; on the twentieth of the month the debate began in the Senate. Immediately Calhoun proposed an amendment to the original proposition, which did not forbid the treasurer from receiving the bills of specie-paying banks, to the effect that all officers of the government should be prohibited from accepting anything in payment of revenue except coin.

[1] Catron to Polk, September 10, 1837, Polk MSS.

[2] Deveraux to Biddle, August 10, 1837; Stilwell to Biddle, September 9, 1837, B.P.; McGrane, *op. cit.*, p. 290.

[3] Jackson to Van Buren, September 14, 1837, Van Buren MSS.

[4] Walker to Polk, September 10, 1837, Polk MSS.

Senator Rives, in behalf of the Conservatives, offered an amendment to continue the present deposit system; and upon these grounds the fight of the giants began. Presumably, three plans were before Congress: one, advocated by Clay and the bank men, was for the re-establishment of a national bank; the second was for the continuance of the present deposit-bank system, with some modifications; and lastly, the Sub-treasury, sanctioned and fathered by Van Buren and the regular Democratic organization.

As the debate progressed, both parties began to shift their original positions. The Democrats, who under Jackson had advocated the deposit scheme, now opposed it; while the Whigs, heretofore violent opponents of the "pet banks," insisted that withdrawal of the public funds from the banks would destroy the financial interests of the land. Proclaiming the increase of executive patronage, the union of sword and the purse, the separation of government from the people, and the injustice to the banks and to the country at large, the Whig cohorts gathered about their leaders. On the opposite side, the Democrats stated the divorce of bank and state would give the treasury full knowledge of its funds, free Congress from bank influence, and restore public confidence in the banks by forcing them to reorganize on a sound financial basis. The most distinguishing feature and the highest recommendation of the proposed system, declared the Democrats, would be the complete and entire separation of the government from all banks. Had not Mr. Biddle, who in the opinion of some, was the greatest financier then living, expressed his opinion in behalf of such an idea? At the organization of the United States Bank of Pennsylvania, in 1836, had he not congratulated the stockholders on the prosperous condition of their interests, the accumulation of a large surplus fund, and the purchase of a new charter, and boasted of the Bank being "safer, stronger, and more prosperous than it ever was?" Had he not added that "it was an original misfortune in the structure of the Bank that it had in any way been connected with persons in office?"[1] Surely here were arguments direct from the camp of the enemy! On one side stood the popular will, the great mass of the people; on the other, the banks and the moneyed power; on the one, the aristocracy of wealth; on the other, the democracy of numbers; here, an alliance of tariff and banking interests; there, friends of the people and the agricultural interests of the nation.[2] The United States Bank was in a remarkable position, and had a remarkable man at its head, ever ready to seize the passing opportunity. If the Sub-treasury bill was defeated, or the measure of Mr. Rives was passed, it would mean restoration to power of the old national

[1] *Cong. Deb.*, **XIV,** Part I, 118.   [2] *Ibid.*, pp. 119, 284.

bank. Therefore, Calhoun, already grown tired of his association with the Whigs, "fearing the renewed danger of the legislative encroachment, and no longer the danger of executive usurpation," pronounced his independent political position by indorsing the Van Buren measure, and by speaking of Jackson as "that great remarkable man."[1] Truly, the Sub-treasury bill was making a strange alignment of political forces in Congress.

Against the arguments of the administration, the Whig senators turned to Tallmadge, Rives, Clay, and Webster for replies. Tallmadge, representing the bank Democratic faction, raised the standard in behalf of the merchants. Why should the people attack the merchants, queried the New York senator. Does not the merchant stand between the government and the consumer? The merchant shoulders the responsibility, and pays into the treasury the enormous revenue which keeps the machinery of government in motion; the merchant maintains the credit of the country abroad. The agricultural interest might be great, but the government will always look to the merchant for the means to aid and defend the latter's interests from outside aggression. Moreover, why were the Democrats so aggressive now for a measure which, when

[1] Blair to Jackson, October 1, 1837, Jackson MSS. For an excellent analysis of Calhoun's motives and actions at this period, consult Cole, *The Whig Party in the South*, pp. 46–49.

first proposed in 1834–35, was signally defeated, and that by the aid of every administration vote save one.[1] Rives taunted Calhoun for his change on the bank question, and rallied the southern Conservatives on the selected state-bank deposit proposal.[2]

But it was left to Clay and Webster to explain fully the Whig position. In two able speeches, the Kentucky senator pointed out the evils of the administration measure; the fact that it would kill the state banks, and make them subservient to the general government; substitute a metalic currency, which "would reduce all property in value two-thirds, thereby forcing every debtor, in effect," to pay three times as much as he had contracted to pay; unite the "sword and the purse," and make the national government too strong.[3] On September 18, Webster rose to defend the national bank, and point out the main criticism of the Sub-treasury bill. The single, undivided, exclusive object of the government bill and the Calhoun amendment was relief for the government; but not a single provision or reference had been made for the relief of the people. But is the government, asked Webster, to care for nothing but itself? "I think not! I think the government exists not for its own ends, but for the public utilities."[4] And in this statement of the

[1] *Cong. Deb.*, XIV, Part I, 162, 171.

[2] *Ibid.*, p. 250.

[3] *Ibid.*, p. 259.   [4] *Cong. Deb.*, XIV, Part I, 314.

situation Webster dealt a blow at the administration defenders.

The party leaders and the people on the outside watched with interest this struggle, commenting on the alliances, and prophesying the ultimate result. The action of the Conservatives especially claimed attention. The *Plaindealer*, a Locofoco organ, asserted that the reason for the division in the Democratic ranks was owing to the people's insistence on the doctrine of equal rights, which the monoply gentry would not acknowledge.[1] In reply, the *Madisonian*, the recognized party spokesman of the Conservatives, announced the principles of the Spartan band resolved to check radical Locofoism as the friends of "union, order, and good faith."[2] But behind all this paper camouflage, the real leaders of the party diagnosed the situation as a presidential plot on the part of Rives and Tallmadge. "Everybody now perceives," wrote Blair to Jackson on October 1, 1837, "that, like Bell's plot about Speaker, there is a presidential plot beneath it." The scheme was that Rives, with Virginia at the head, was to carry off the whole South. Tallmadge, with the bank power, it was supposed, would be able to make up a mixed party that would, with Whiggery, carry a majority in the money and trading regions. So that the two to-

[1] *Plaindealer*, July 15, 1837.

[2] *Madisonian*, September 30, 1837.

gether, as president and vice-president, being the candidates of the opposition (Clay, Webster, and Harrison being disposed of), could put an end to Mr. Van Buren at the close of the first session.[1] Undoubtedly this was correct; and Biddle and his followers, seeing the advisability of keeping the Democratic ranks divided, had early sanctioned this move.[2] A month before Congress assembled, a friend of the United States Bank had visited Saratoga Springs with the purpose of conferring with Tallmadge, in order to line up the members-elect to Congress to sustain him in his course and arrange for meetings in various sections of the state to uphold these liberal measures.[3] Six days after Congress convened, another adherent of the Bank wrote Tallmadge, advising him of the most popular method to adopt in order to defeat the Sub-treasury bill; while on the same day Biddle was congratulated on the disunion among the Democrats, and the belief that the Conservatives would go with the Whigs.[4] But when it came to placing Tallmadge and Rives at the head of the ticket, the Whigs

[1] Blair to Jackson, October 1, 1837, Jackson MSS.

[2] This does not mean to imply that Biddle favored such a plot, or was even cognizant of the scheme. But it is correct to say that Biddle, as did all the bank men, saw the advantage to the Whigs of allying with the Conservatives. There is proof, in the Biddle Papers, of the bankers' interest in the Conservative party.

[3] Devereaux to Biddle, August 10, 1837, B.P.

[4] McGrane, *op. cit.*, p. 290.

objected.[1] They were willing to receive them into their ranks, but only on terms that they fall in at the rear. Therefore, the Conservatives failed to answer the purpose of the Whigs, for on the final vote in the Senate on October 4, the bill passed by a vote of twenty-six to twenty.[2]

The debate in the House began on the tenth; and here the sectional lines were more strongly drawn than in the Senate. The opening speech made by Pickens, of South Carolina, laid out the lines of the combat. Arguing in favor of an Independent Treasury, the South Carolinian raised the contention that the organization of the banking power of the country connected with the government tended to make the labor of the exporting districts tributary to the banking capital by their control of the credit and banking power. Then, in reply to the statement of Cushing of Massachusetts, that the "progress of radicalism at the North was nothing more than the progress of abolitionism," Pickens launched into a defense of slavery. "We own nearly one-half of our population. . . . . We are interested in the bona fide profits of daily labor, for we own not only the proceeds of labor but labor itself. . . . . We are then,

[1] Blair to Jackson, October 1, 1837, Jackson MSS.

[2] The vote in the Senate showed the strength of the administration. The bill passed by a strict administration vote, with but one Whig voting for the passage of the measure. The Whig member was Niles, of Connecticut.

in fact, capitalists standing in the place of laborers, and are, to all intents and purposes, laborers. . . . . The laborers of the non-slave-holding states are interested also in the bona fide . . . . profits of daily labor." Yet capital is holding down labor in the North. Therefore, "when gentlemen preach up, as they have done for the last three years, insurrection to the slaves of our community, I warn them that their own institutions are not so pure as they might at first suppose, and that I will preach up insurrection to the laborers of the North." If the North declares this is Locofocoism, "I tell them I proclaim the doctrines of Jefferson, that the democracy of the North are the natural allies of the South."[1] The speech of Pickens fell as a bomb in the midst of the assembly; the fear of the alliance of the Locofoco element of the North with the southern planter would mean the complete overthrow of the banking power and the establishment of the southern cotton supremacy.

The Whigs hastened to reply. Calhoun of Massachusetts, in answer to Pickens' charge, declared that the southern representative did not understand the labor of the North, or the nature of its banking institutions or other corporations. They were not engaged "in enslaving and subjecting the laboring class." They were themselves the laboring class— the men of business of the great middle class of

[1] *Cong. Deb.*, XIV, Part II, October 10, 1837, p. 1394.

society, the men who by their industry and intellect
had made themselves what they were. The banking institutions were owned, not by the great
capitalists, but by the active, thriving, energetic
men of business. The ownerships of the corporations were for the most part in the hands of men
of moderate property, of females, of orphans, of
charitable institutions.[1] However, when Moore of
New York, a Democrat with Locofoco leanings, confirmed Pickens' charges against capitalists of the
North,[2] the opposition grew more determined to
repudiate the accusation, and break up the threatened alliance. Naylor of Pennyslvania repudiated
the word "capitalist," claiming that all men were
laborers in the North. The characteristics of capitalist and laborer were united in one person in the
North. The man who was a "capitalist" had become so by his industry and perseverance. He had
begun as a humble laborer; his industry, virtue, and
integrity had been his only capital. Such was
Stephen Girard, the merchant, who had begun his
career as a destitute cabin-boy; Governor Ritner,
the wagoner; James Todd, the attorney-general of
Pennsylvania, a woodchopper; and numerous other
so-called "wealthy leaders."[3] Still fearful of the
extent of the havoc wrought by Pickens' utterances,
the Whigs turned to the Conservatives.[4] Here they

[1] *Op. cit.*, p. 1470.   [3] *Op. cit.*, p. 1575.
[2] *Op. cit.*, p. 1587.   [4] *Op. cit.*, p. 1486.

received the desired help, especially from the Virginia contingent, and as the debate drew to a close, the friends of the measure saw that the southern followers of Calhoun had failed to break the power of the moneyed interests. The day before the final vote, Blair wrote:

The friends of the administration in the House are laboring with all zeal to keep the sneaking and dodging Bank Democrats to their posts tonight (it is now nine o'clock), that they may get the Divorce Bill out of the Committee of the Whole. I am apprehensive that treachery is too much intended to compass it. The Conservatives are every moment dodging off into a committee room, where it is said Rives and Tallmadge have a little conservatory, and ply them with all sorts of good words and winning ways to induce them to lay the bill over to the next session. . . . . The two senators hope something from time and a new impetus from the banks.[1]

A few days later Blair announced the postponement of the measure, due to the aid given the Whigs by the Virginia Conservatives.[2] By a vote of 119 to 107, the Whigs had shifted the contest on to the next session of Congress.[3]

[1] Blair to Jackson, October 13, 1837, Jackson MSS.

[2] Blair to Jackson, October 15, 1837, Jackson MSS.

[3] The vote resulted in ninety-three Whigs, twenty-one Van Buren men, and five with no political party designations voting in favor of tabling the bill. Cf. comments on final vote in the *Globe*, October 14, 1837; Niles, October 21, 1837; *National Intelligencer*, October 21, 1837; Buchanan to Jackson, October 26, 1837, Jackson MSS.

The December message of the President returned to the subject, undaunted by the late defeat. But the former contest had taught Van Buren the need of compromise. Thus the tone of the measure was more conciliatory toward state banks, and intimated that if the majority of Congress could not agree with the original proposal, a suitable substitute might be found in its stead.[1] This section was referred to Senator Wright, as chairman of the Finance Committee, and on January 16 a bill, including Calhoun's former amendment of the "specie clause," was presented to the Senate. Rives, on behalf of the third party, proposed a substitute midway between the national bank and the Independent Treasury, by selecting twenty-five banks as public depositories; and around these measures the Senate resumed its titanic struggle.

However, the debate in this session did not present many new attractions over that of the former discussion. Calhoun urged haste; Clay advised delay. Tallmadge once more got in touch with Biddle, and sought new arguments against the Subtreasury bill from the Philadelphia financier.[2] Clay taunted Calhoun for aiding the enemy, while the latter referred to the historic Adams-Clay coalition as a precedent. Senators on both sides tried to interpret the fall elections, undoubtedly satisfac-

[1] Richardson, *Messages and Papers of the Presidents*, III, 382.
[2] Colt to Biddle, January 24, 1838, B.P.

torily to themselves and their friends, but without convincing their opponents.[1] The followers of the South Carolina senator hurled their familiar darts against the national bank and the Rives bill as a proposal leading to the installation of the moneyed power,[2] while the opposition poured forth the accustomed violent and bitter denunciations against Locofocoism and agrarianism.

But the fate of the measure was not decided in the Senate; the controlling force came from without, and came from the seat of the opposition—Nicholas Biddle. During the previous debate of 1837, the Conservative senators had not rendered the desired aid in obstructing the administration as Biddle hoped they would. Now the careful financier turned to Clay, as the leader of the bank men, to command the forces, while the master-mind at Philadelphia directed the maneuvers. Whigs and Democrats realized that the vote would be close, and therefore additional diligence would be necessary to secure its passage or destruction. Polk, Grundy, Buchanan, and Kendall[3] felt confident of the success, though acknowledging that the majority might be small; while Yell and Calhoun doubted the final outcome.

[1] *Cong. Globe, Twenty-fifth Cong., Second Sess.*, App., pp. 98, 166, 167.

[2] *Ibid.*, App., p. 193.

[3] Polk to Jackson, January 4(?), 1838; Grundy to Jackson, January 29, 1838, Jackson MSS; Buchanan to———, January 13, 1838, Buchanan MSS; McGrane, *op. cit.*, p. 297.

Clay, Webster and the bank friends at Washington likewise informed Biddle that the vote would favor themselves.[1] But while both sides were trying to figure out the count to a nicety, Biddle was acting.

The plan adopted was to get the state legislatures to instruct their senators to vote against the measure, and four days after the debate began in the Senate, Biddle set to work on this scheme. On February 3 he wrote to Clay in the following confidential manner: "You may readily suppose that we are not idle while this insane Sub-treasury scheme is urged forward to break down all the great interests of the country. Preparations are made to obtain from our legislature at Harrisburg instructions to our representatives in Congress to oppose it." These would be introduced into the state legislature at once. Therefore, continuing in the same strain, Biddle concluded his note to Clay: "I lose no time, therefore, in suggesting that you would keep up the debate in the Senate for a few days until the resolutions can reach you. I attach great importance to this measure as separating our state from these desperadoes, and the country looks to you eminently to exert your great powers as they have been so often displayed for its protection."[2] The next day the financier wrote again to Clay, urging

[1] McGrane, *op. cit.*, pp. 297, 298; cf. also Van Tyne, *Webster Letters*, p. 211.

[2] McGrane, *op. cit.*, p. 299.

him to get Buchanan to take a definite stand on the position of instructions, and to encourage him to declare his intention to resign on receipt of resolutions of which he disapproved. Clay replied immediately on the receipt of these letters, rejoicing in the movement under contemplation, and assuring the bank president that "the final question would *not* be taken that week." The next day Clay communicated that he had met Buchanan at a small party, and rallied him on the subject of instruction, and that the latter had intimated his intention either to obey or resign if they came, preferably the former. "I do not think an occasion will present itself," wrote Clay, "but if it does I will embrace it to draw from Mr. B. a more explicit declaration."[1] The opportunity came that very day, while discussing the instructions for Grundy, of Tennessee. Clay seized upon it to declare in the Senate his hope that if the senator from Pennsylvania received similar instructions he would be guilty of no evasion, "but meet them boldly, and either obey them or resign and go home."[2]

Haste was essential, for Calhoun was moving "heaven and earth," as Webster said,[3] to obtain southern votes for the measure by convincing his southern friends that its success would relieve them

[1] *Ibid.*, p. 300.

[2] *Cong. Globe, Twenty-fifth Cong., Second Sess.*, p. 166.

[3] McGrane, *op. cit.*, p. 301.

from their commercial dependence on the North. Biddle turned his whole attention, therefore, to Harrisburg, where the fight was being carried on by C. S. Baker, in charge of the bank forces against the Democratic forces. From the seventh to the sixteenth, the contest continued, the Democrats trying to thwart the Whigs' project by constantly calling for yeas and nays while the Whigs endeavored to keep their men in line.

At last, on the sixteenth, the resolutions were passed, and on the nineteenth Buchanan presented them in the Senate, and gave his adhesion. "We now probably stand twenty-six against twenty-six," wrote Clay to Biddle. "One more vote will defeat the vile measure."[1] But to secure that extra vote required a month's debate, during which time Van Buren and the Democrats forecasted the passage of the bill by the deciding vote of the vice-president.[2] The final vote was, however, twenty-seven to twenty-five, Calhoun voting in the negative because of the fact that his specie clause had been stricken out.[3]

[1] McGrane, *op. cit.*, pp. 302-5.

[2] Van Buren to Jackson, March 17, 1838, Van Buren MSS. Cf. also Colt to Biddle, February 26, 1838, containing the same statements.

[3] Benton, *Thirty Years' View*, II, 124, on Calhoun's vote. The vote at this session, like the former ballot, was a strict administration vote; only one Whig voted in favor of the measure: Niles, of Connecticut.

Biddle's work had again proved futile, undoubtedly owing to the southerners' jealousy of the northerners. As Sergeant stated, they had supported the Independent Treasury in order to get their own trade into their own hands. The mass of them had been sincere; Calhoun had used it "only to cloak his ambition."[1]

The defeat of the Whigs in the Senate was a blow to Biddle's plans, but before the measure came up in the House, in which Calhoun doubted its ultimate passage, circumstances were to play into the bank party's hands, and place them in a most favorable position for combating the administration. On May 30 the Specie Circular was repealed in the Senate by a vote of 34 to 9, and in the House by 154 to 29. Straightway Clay informed Biddle of the glad tidings, urging at the same time the immediate resumption of specie payment, which, up to this period, the United States Bank had opposed. Such a procedure, stated Clay, would turn aside all the malignant attacks on the Bank; perhaps reconcile the public ultimately to the grant of a national charter.[2] Biddle saw the wisdom of this, and immediately moved toward resumption.[3]

---

[1] McGrane, *op. cit.*, pp. 305–7.

[2] Biddle to Jaudon, May 31, 1838, B.P. For Webster's account of the origin of the motion to repeal the Specie Circular, cf. McGrane, *op. cit.*, pp. 310, 311.

[3] Cf. previous chapter.

Nevertheless, the fight was not over. The House still had to decide the fate of the Senate bill. The first glimpse of sunshine was soon dispelled by the administration forces rallying to the attack. The House, unfavorably disposed to the Senate's actions on the specie clause, refused to consider the measure, and for a week delayed the debate on the subject. Each day's delay lessened its chance of passage, so declared the bank men, and yet the administration could not bring it forward on account of the difficulty over the specie clause.[1] At last Cambreleng introduced a new bill, which the administration determined to push through the House. Sergeant immediately went to Philadelphia to consult Biddle; agents were sent by the United States Bank to Washington to explain to the representatives from Pennsylvania how to defeat the new project. So imminent seemed the danger that Biddle asked Sergeant for a list of all those who would vote against it, and also how many votes were needed in addition. "Perhaps we may prove to some of our Pennsylvania members that their course is injurious to the state and to themselves," significantly wrote the financier. The real secret of the bill, declared Biddle, was that Calhoun was driving the unwilling mass of the administration to pass it in order to promote his own advance-

[1] Sergeant to Biddle, July 4, 1838; Connell to Biddle, July 6, 1838, B.P.

ment.[1] If this were true, it failed of its purpose, for on June 25 the House negatived the measure (125 to 111), and a motion to reconsider was routed by 205 to 121.[2] Thus the measure was disposed of for the session of 1838.

Biddle claimed the whole glory for the victory. "Remember," exultantly wrote Biddle to Jaudon on the twenty-ninth, "that whatever you may read to the contrary, the repeal of the Specie Circular and the defeat of the Sub-treasury are the results, exclusively, of a course pursued by the Bank of the United States. If we had done as the New York banks had, succumbed to the government and resumed when they did, it would have been a surrender. . . . . I was willing to risk the temporary overshadowing to have a permanent sunshine, and I think we shall soon have it."[3]

Unquestionably the stand taken by the Bank in refusing so long to resume specie payment, and thus placing the administration on the defensive for over a year, had contributed to the checking of Van Buren's plans. By the aid of the Conservatives, Biddle had worked havoc with the first bill; by his own machinations he had brought about the second defeat. On July 9 Congress adjourned, with the

---

[1] McGrane, *op. cit.*, p. 314.

[2] Those voting to negative the bill were one hundred Whigs, eighteen Democrats, and seven of no political party designations.

[3] McGrane, *op. cit.*, p. 315.

administration leaders still insisting they would bring the Independent Treasury forward in the next session.

With unfaltering steadfastness Van Buren returned to the struggle in his December message of 1839. The nation was already in the throes of another panic. The collapse of the United States Bank had destroyed its former prestige. Moreover, there was no longer a Biddle to guide the finances of the country, or check the government in its last attempt to pass the Independent Treasury.

Much depended on the organization of the House and the complexion of the Senate. When Congress assembled on December 2, 1839, there were 121 Democrats and 113 Whigs in the House, with a double delegation from New Jersey claiming seats. After a period of great confusion, R. M. T. Hunter, a States Rights man, but favorable to the Independent Treasury, was chosen speaker; and the House decided to seat the five Democratic representatives, thereby giving the Democrats 126 votes and the Whigs 115.[1] With the House in their control, five vacancies in the Senate,[2] and the panic of 1839 to arouse the people against the banks, the

---

[1] On the election of speaker and the political maneuvering on the subject, cf. J. Q. Adams, *Memoirs*, X, 144, 148; Jameson, *Correspondence of Calhoun*, pp. 435, 437; Blair to Jackson, December 15, 1839; Blair to Jackson, December 22, 1839, Jackson MSS.

[2] The vacancies at this time were from New York, Pennsylvania, Delaware, Virginia, and Arkansas.

administration resolved to push rapidly the Independent Treasury, before the Whigs could bring the state legislatures to instruct their men to vote against the bill.

Accordingly, on January 14, Wright of New York presented the bill to the Senate. The familiar arguments so often explained since 1837 were reiterated by friend and foe. Clay made the only speech of importance, on January 20, in behalf of the bank cause:

Whilst all the elements of destruction are at work, and the storm is raging, the Chief Magistrate, standing in the midst of his unprotected fellow-citizens . . . . deliberately wraps around himself the folds of his Indian-rubber cloak, and lifting his umbrella over his head, tells them . . . . that he means to take care of himself. . . . . For ten long years we have been waring against the alarming growth of executive power, but although we have been occasionally cheered, it has been constantly advancing, and never receding. . . . . The insatiable spirit of the Stuarts for power and prerogative was brought upon our American throne on the fourth of March, 1829. It came under all the usual false and hypocritical pretense and disguises of love of the people, desire for reform, and diffidence of power. The Scotch dynasty still continues. We have had Charles I, and now have Charles II, but I again thank God that our deliverance is at hand, and that on March 4, 1841, a great and glorious revolution, without blood and without convulsion, will be achieved.[1]

But neither the oratory of the western senator nor instructions from state legislatures could stem

[1] *Cong. Globe, Twenty-sixth Cong., First Sess.,* App., pp. 726–31.

the tide. On January 23 the bill passed the Senate.[1]

With the House in the hands of the administration, the bill seemed fated to pass. But still the opposition struggled against its enactment. Insisting upon the maintenance of the rules which placed private and unimportant bills before the Subtreasury on the calendar, continually delaying legislation by speech-making, and by constantly leaving the hall and thereby breaking the quorum, the Whig leaders strove to stave off the passage of the bill.[2] In utter despair, Blair wrote to Jackson, recounting the conditions of the House and the utter futility of securing a final vote.[3] The appeal aroused the old warrior to the danger threatening the administration measure, and he exclaimed against the situation:

It is humiliating to think that a majority of the Democratic members in Congress would permit themselves to be governed by a minority in the opposition. They ought, like faithful soldiers, to unite and be at their posts, and pass the Independent Treasury bill before one moves from his post. You may assure them that if they do not, the denunciation of the democracy will be loud and strong all over the Union. It will not be received as an excuse that the opposition members have succeeded, when they have a constitutional number to coerce the attendance of absent members—such a precedent would dissolve the government, and the blame will

[1] The vote was strictly administration, not a single Whig voting in favor of the bill.

[2] *Globe*, May 18, 21, 1840.

[3] Blair to Jackson, June 17, 18 (?), Jackson MSS.

be laid at their door—they ought to look to it and permit no leave of absence until this bill is passed upon. If they do, it will be like a general on the lines of an enemy, who gives his soldiers furloughs until he becomes so weak that the enemy sallies forth, defeats, and destroys him, for will not a precedent that the minority rules, destroy our representative government? Let the majority look to it, sit it out, no more be absent, and when the floor is not occupied, move that the committee rise and report the bill to the House, and carry it, and then, by the previous question, pass the bill. If the opposition attempt to leave the House to prevent a quorum, let there be a roll call of the House, and by the sergeant-at-arms coerce their attendance. It is not for the democracy to use delicate or usual courtesy to those who have combined to destroy our government, nor will the democracy of the country excuse them on such a plea.[1]

Thus impelled by the sage at Nashville, and whipped into line by blasts from the *Globe*, the Democrats remained at their stations, and at last, on June 30, three days after Jackson had written the above letter, the bill passed the House by 123 to 99 nays.[2]

On July 4, 1840, the Independent Treasury became the law of the land. The resumption of specie payment in 1838 had been the epilogue of the panic of 1837, and the prologue of the panic of 1839; while the long strife over resumption and the Independent Treasury bill, by disclosing the dictatorial methods

[1] Jackson to Blair, June 27, 1840, Jackson MSS.

[2] For Whig explanations of the result, cf. McMaster, *History of the United States*, VI, 548.

of Nicholas Biddle and the later extravagant transactions of the banks, brought about the destruction
of the "moneyed autocracy" that Jackson had
assayed in 1832. Not until 1844, however, did the
currency attain a state of perfect soundness;[1] but
ere this had taken place Nicholas Biddle had died,
and the people's attention had been diverted to new
problems too long obscured by this internecine
contest.

[1] A partial resumption took place in June, 1842, but the
trouble was not over until 1844. Cf. *Hunt's Merchants' Magazine*,
VII, 78, 79; *ibid.*, X, pp. 75, 560; Richardson, *Messages and Papers*,
IV, 352.

BIBLIOGRAPHY

I. MANUSCRIPTS

The following manuscripts are found in the Library of Congress, Pennsylvania Historical Society Library, Wisconsin Historical Society Library, New York Public Library, and Harvard University Library. All titles in the bibliography are arranged alphabetically.

BIDDLE PAPERS, 1830–44

This is an invaluable source for the period. It contains excellent material on the social, political, and economic phases of the Jacksonian area. Pertinent extracts are published in McGrane, R. C., *Correspondence of Nicholas Biddle* (Boston, 1919).

BIDDLE PRESIDENT'S LETTER BOOKS, 1830–40

Biddle's books as president of the Bank.

GREEN BAY AND PRAIRIE DU CHIEN MANUSCRIPTS

JAMES H. HAMMOND PAPERS, 1835-38

Excellent for politics in the southern states.

ANDREW JACKSON PAPERS, 1833–40

Indispensable for the Jacksonian era.

BISHOP JACKSON KEMPER'S LETTER BOOK, DIARY, PAPERS

These manuscripts contain a wealth of information on all subjects dealing with the conditions in the West.

WILLIAM L. MARCY PAPERS, 1834–40

An excellent collection of papers on New York politics. Especially valuable on the Locofoco movement in that state.

MORGAN L. MARTIN PAPERS

Martin, with Solomon Juneau, was one of the founders of Milwaukee.

NEW YORK AND MISSISSIPPI LAND COMPANY PAPERS

JOEL R. POINSETT PAPERS, 1836–38

JAMES K. POLK PAPERS, 1835–40

Good for politics in Tennessee and land operation in the South.

MOSES M. STRONG PAPERS

Strong was a surveyor and land agent for a number of wealthy eastern investors. Throughout the collection are scattered a number of letters which throw much light on land speculation during these years.

MARTIN VAN BUREN PAPERS, 1833–40

Invaluable for politics and economics during this period.

Useful scattering materials have been found in the following collections of manuscripts: William Allen, James Buchanan, Salmon P. Chase, John Crittenden, Flagg, Chancellor Kent, Duncan McArthur, John McLean, Sumner, Stevenson, and Wolf.

II. NEWSPAPERS

The Age, 1838

Albany Argus, 1837–40

Albany Journal, 1837–40

Alton Telegraph, 1836, 1837

American Sentinel, 1836

Baltimore Merchant Journal, 1837–38

Baltimore Reporter and Commercial Advertiser, 1837

Boston Bay State, 1839

Boston Chronicle and Patriot, 1836–39

Boston Evening Mercantile Journal, 1838

Chicago American, 1835–37

Cincinnati Daily Gazette, 1836–42

Cincinnati Enquirer, 1836

Financial Register, Vols. I, II

Frankfort Commonwealth, 1837

Galena Advertiser, 1838

Keystone (Philadelphia), 1836

Lowell Courier, 1836–38

The Madisonian, 1837–38

The Man, 1834

Maysville Eagle, 1832–38

National Intelligencer, 1832–40

New Hampshire Patriot, 1838

The New Era, 1837–38

New Haven Daily Herald, 1839

New York Courier and Enquirer, 1835

New York Evening Post, 1836

New York Evening Star, 1838

New York Journal of Commerce, 1836–40
New York Spectator, 1837
New York Times, 1836–38
Niles Register, 1830–40
Ohio Statesman, 1837, 1838
Pennsylvanian, 1836
Philadelphia Advertiser, 1837, 1838
Philadelphia Courier, 1836
Philadelphia National Gazette, 1837–42
Plaindealer, 1836
Radical Reformer, 1835
Richmond Enquirer, 1836–40
Sangamon Journal, 1836
United States Telegraph, 1836
Vermont Argus, 1837
Vermont Gazette, 1838
Washington Globe, 1830–42
Worcester (Massachusetts) *Spy*, 1838
Worcester Palladium, 1838, 1839
Worcester Ohio Republican Advocate, 1837–38
Zenia Torchlight, 1838

MEMOIRS, CORRESPONDENCE, SPEECHES, AND WORKS

ADAMS, J. Q. *Memoirs*, Philadelphia, 1876, 12 Vols.

BAKER, G. E. (editor). *Works of W. H. Seward*, New York, 1853, 5 Vols.

BENTON, T. H. *Thirty Years' View*, New York, 1854, 2 Vols.

COLTON, C. *Private Correspondence of Henry Clay*, Cincinnati, 1856

COLTON, C. *Works of Henry Clay*, New York, 1904, 10 Vols.

DEARBORN, H. A. S. *Letters on the Internal Improvements and Commerce of the West*, Boston, 1839

GREELEY, H. *Recollections of a Busy Life*, New York, 1868

JAMESON, J. F. (editor). "Correspondence of John C. Calhoun," in *American Historical Association Report*, 1899, Vol. II, Washington, 1900

MOORE, J. D. (editor). *Works of James Buchanan*, Philadelphia, 1908, 12 Vols.

SEWARD, F. W. *W. H. Seward, an Autobiography*, New York, 1891, 3 Vols.

TRUMBLE, A. *Autobiography and Correspondence of*, in Old Northwest Genealogical Society, 1909

TYLER, L. G. *Letters and Times of the Tylers*, Richmond and Williamsburg, 1884–96, 3 Vols.

VAN TYNE, C. H. (editor). *Letters of Daniel Webster*, New York, 1902

WEBSTER, F. (editor). *Private Correspondence of Daniel Webster*, Boston, 1857

WEED, H. A. *Autobiography of Thurlow Weed*, Boston, 1884

WOODBURY, L. *Writings, Political, Judicial, and Literary*, Boston, 1842, 3 Vols.

BIOGRAPHIES

AMBLER, C. H. *Thomas Ritchie: a Study of Virginia Politics*, Richmond, 1913

BANCROFT, F. *Life of W. H. Seward*, New York, 1900, 2 Vols.

CUTLER, J. T. *Life and Times of Ephraim Cutler*, Cincinnati, 1890

HALE, E. E. *W. H. Seward*, Philadelphia, 1910

JARVIS, E. *Autobiography*

JERVEY, T. D. *Robert Y. Hayne and His Times*, New York, 1909

KONKLE, B. A. *Life and Speeches of Thomas Williams*, Philadelphia, 1905, 2 Vols.

McCORMAC, E. I. *James K. Polk: a Political Biography*, Berkeley, 1922

MACKENZIE, W. L. *Life and Opinions of Benjamin S. Butler and Jesse Hoyt*, Boston, 1845

PHILLIPS, U. B. *Life of Robert Toombs*, New York, 1913

REYNOLDS, J. *My Own Times*, 1879

SCHURZ, C. *Henry Clay*, Boston, 1898, 2 Vols.

SNYDER, J. F. *A. W. Snyder*, Springfield, 1903

SUMNER, W. G. *Andrew Jackson*, Boston, 1898

DIARIES AND TRAVELS

CHEVALIER, M. *Society, Manners and Politics in the United States*, Boston, 1839

GRUND, F. J. *The Americans in their Moral, Social, and Political Relations*, London, 1837, 2 Vols.

HALL, J. *Statistics of the West*, Cincinnati, 1836

MARRYAT, F. A. *Diary in America*, Philadelphia, 1839

MARTINEAU, H. *Society in America*, London, 1837, 2 Vols.

TUCKERMAN, B. (editor), *Diary of Philip Hone*, New York, 1910, 2 Vols.

PUBLIC DOCUMENTS: FEDERAL

American State Papers, Land, Vol. VII

Circular to Register and Recorders in Chief Clerk's Office, Land Office, Washington, D.C.

Congressional Debates, 1830–36

Congressional Globe, 1837–40

Commissioner of Labor Report, 1886

Secretary of Treasury Report, 1830–40, in *Congressional Documents*

United States Census, 1830, 1840, 1880

Twelfth Census Statistical Atlas

Executive Documents, Twenty-second Cong., Second Sess., Docs. 105, 165

Executive Documents, Twenty-third Cong., Second Sess., Doc. 190

Executive Documents, Twenty-fifth Cong., Second Sess., Docs. 79, 80

Executive Documents, Twenty-fifth Cong., Third Sess., Doc. 172

Senate Documents, Twenty-fifth Cong., Second Sess., Doc. 471

Senate Documents, Twenty-fifth Cong., Third Sess., Doc. 31

STATE DOCUMENTS

Arkansas Journal of General Assembly, 1837–42

Delaware Senate Journal, 1837–42

Florida Journal of Proceedings of Legislative Council and Senate, 1837–44

Georgia Senate and House Journal, 1837–44

Illinois Senate and House Journal and Reports to House and Senate, 1837–44

Indiana Senate Journal and Senate Documents, 1837–44

Kentucky Senate and House Journal, 1837–44; *Legislative Documents*, 1837–41

Louisiana Senate and House Journal, 1837–44

Maryland Senate Journal, 1837–44

Massachusetts Senate and House Journal, and Legislative Documents, 1837–44

Michigan Senate Journal and Documents, 1837–44

Mississippi Senate and House Journal, 1837–44

Missouri Senate and House Journal, 1837–44

New Hampshire Senate Journal, 1837–44

New Jersey General Assembly, 1837–44

New York Senate and House Journal and Assembly Documents, 1837–44

North Carolina Senate and House Journal and Legislative Documents, 1837–44

Ohio Senate Journal and Legislative Documents, 1837–44

Pennsylvania Senate and House Journal, 1837–44

*South Carolina Proceedings of Senate and House and
    Reports and Resolutions of General Assembly,*
    1837–44
Tennessee Senate and House Journal, 1837–44
Vermont Senate and House Journal, 1837–44
Virginia Journal of House of Delegates, 1837–44

STATE STATUTES

Statutes of the following states, from 1837 to
1842: Arkansas, Connecticut, Delaware, Florida,
Georgia, Illinois, Indiana, Kentucky, Louisiana,
Maine, Maryland, Massachusetts, Michigan, Miss-
issippi, Missouri, New Hampshire, New Jersey,
New York, North Carolina, Ohio, Pennsylvania,
Rhode Island, South Carolina, Tennessee, Vermont,
Virginia.

SPECIAL ARTICLES, WORKS, AND
MONOGRAPHS

ALEXANDER, DE A. S. *A Political History of the
    State of New York,* New York, 1906
AMBLER, C. H. *Sectionalism in Virginia from 1776
    to 1861,* Chicago, 1910
ATWATER, C. *History of the State of Ohio,* Cin-
    cinnati, 1838
BISHOP, A. L. *The State Works of Pennsylvania,* in
    Connecticut Academy of Arts and Science,
    Vol. XIII
BISHOP, J. L. *A History of American Manufactures,
    1608 to 1860,* Philadelphia, 1864, 2 Vols.

BOGART, E. L. *Financial History of Ohio*, Urbana, 1912

BOURNE, E. G. *Distribution of the Surplus Revenue of 1837*, New York, 1885

BRYAN, A. C. *State Banking in Maryland*, in "Johns Hopkins Studies," Series 17, Nos. 1–3

BURTON, T. E. *Financial Crises*, New York, 1903

BYRSDALL, F. *History of the Loco Foco or Equal Rights Party*, New York, 1842.

CARLTON, F. T. "The Workingmen's Party of New York City, 1829 to 1831," in *Political Science Quarterly*, XXII, 401–16

CATTERALL, R. C. H. *Second Bank of the United States*, Chicago, 1903

CLARK, V. S. *History of Manufactures in the United States, 1607 to 1860*, Washington, 1916

COLE, A. C. *The Whig Party in the South*, Washington, 1913

COMMONS, C. R. *History of Labor in the United States*, New York, 1918, 2 Vols.

COMMONS, C. R. *Documentary History of American Industrial Society*, Cleveland, 1910, 7 Vols.

DARLING, A. B. "Jacksonian Democracy in Massachusetts, 1824 to 1848," in *American Historical Review*, January, 1924, pp. 271–88

DAVIDSON, A. and STRUVE, B. *A Complete History of Illinois, 1673 to 1873*, Springfield, 1874

DEWEY, D. R. *The Second Bank of the United States*, Washington, 1910

DEWEY, D. R. *State Banking before the Civil War*, Washington, 1910

DOUBLEDAY, T. *A Financial, Monetary, and Statistical History of England*, London, 1846

DUDEN, M. "Internal Improvements in Indiana, 1816 to 1846," in *Indiana Quarterly Magazine of History*, December, 1909

ESAREY, L. "Internal Improvements in Early Indiana," in *Indiana Historical Society Publications*, Vol. V, No. 2

ESAREY, L. "State Banking in Indiana," in *Indiana University Studies*, No. 1

FISH, C. R. *Civil Service and the Patronage*, New York, 1905

FORD, T. *History of Illinois*, Chicago, 1854

FOX, D. R. *Decline of Aristocracy in the Politics of New York*, New York, 1919

FULLER, G. N. *Economic and Social Beginnings of Michigan*, in "Michigan Historical Publications, University Series," No. 1

GEPHART, W. F. *Transportation and Industrial Growth in the Middle West*, in "Columbia University Studies," Vol. XXXIV

GOUGE, W. M. *The Curse of Paper Money and Banking*, London, 1833

GROSS, L. M. *Past and Present of De Kalb County, Illinois*, Chicago, 1907

HADLEY, A. T. *Railway Transportation*, New York, 1903

HALL, G. H. *Industrial Depression*, New York, 1911

HAMMOND, J. D. *History of Political Parties in New York*, Syracuse, 1852

HANEY, L. H. *Congressional History of Railroads in the United States to 1850*, in "University of Wisconsin Bulletins," Vol. III

HARDING, W. F. "State Banking in Indiana, 1834 to 1859," in *Journal of Political Economy*, December, 1905

HAZARD, B. E. *The Organization of the Boot and Shoe Industry of Massachusetts before 1875*, Boston, 1921

HILDRETH, R. *Banks, Banking, and Paper Currency*, Boston, 1840

HILL, H. W. "Historical Review of Waterways and Canals in New York State," in *Publications of Buffalo Historical Society*, Vol. XII

HUNTINGTON, C. C. "A History of Banking and Currency in Ohio before the Civil War," in *Ohio Arch. and Hist. Soc. Pub.*, Vol. XXIV

HUNTINGTON, C. C. and MCCLELLAND, C. P. *History of Ohio Canals*, Columbus, 1905

JENKINS, J. S. *History of Political Parties in New York*, Auburn, 1849

JUGLAR, C. *A Brief History of Panics*, New York, 1893

KEITH, H. E. "Historical Sketch of Internal Improvements in Michigan, 1836 to 1846," in *Pub. Pol. Sci. Assoc.*, Vol. IV

KINLEY, D. *The Independent Treasury*, Washington, 1910

KLEIN, T. B. "Canals of Pennsylvania," in *Annual Rep. of Sec. of Internal Affairs of Pennsylvania*, 1900

LEWIS, A. *The Rise of the American Proletariat*, Chicago, 1907

LINCOLN, C. Z. *Constitutional History of New York*, Rochester, 1905–8

McCULLOCK, J. R. *A Dictionary . . . . of Commerce and Commercial Navigation*, London, 1882

MARTIN, W. E. *Internal Improvements in Alabama*, in "Johns Hopkins Studies," Vol. XX

MATSON, N. *Reminiscences of Bureau County*, Princeton, Illinois, 1872

MEYER, B. H. *History of Transportation in the United States before 1860*, Washington, 1917

MORRIS, C. N. "Internal Improvements in Ohio, 1825–30," in *Amer. Hist. Assoc. Papers*, Vol. III

MOSES, J. *Illinois Historical and Statistical*, Chicago, 1889, 2 Vols.

MYERS, G. *History of Tammany Hall*, New York, 1901

PEASE, T. C. *A Frontier State, 1818–48*, Springfield, 1918

PHILLIPS, U. B. "Georgia and States Rights," in *Amer. Hist. Assoc. Rep.*, Vol. I.

PHILLIPS, U. B. *A Southern Whig in Turner Essays*, New York, 1910

PHILLIPS, U. B. *Transportation in the Eastern Cotton Belt to 1860*, New York, 1908

PITKIN, T. *Statistical Review of the Commerce of the United States*, New Haven, 1835

POOLEY, W. V. *A Settlement of Illinois, 1830–50*, Madison, 1908

POOR, H. V. *History of the Railroads and Canals of the United States*, New York, 1860

POOR, H. V. *Sketch of the Rise and Progress of Internal Improvements*, New York, 1881

PORTER, R. T. *The West from the Census of 1880*, Chicago, 1882

POWELL, T. E. *The Democratic Party of Ohio*, Columbus, 1913

RAGUET, C. *A Treatise on Currency and Banking*, London, 1839

REIZENSTEIN, M. *Economic History of the Baltimore and Ohio Railroad*, in "Johns Hopkins Studies," Vol. XV

REYNER, I. *On the Crises of 1837 and 1857*, in "University of Nebraska Studies," Vol. V

SCOTT, W. A. *Repudiation of State Debts*, New York, 1893

SHELTON, H. H. "Bankruptcy Law, Its History and Purpose," in *Amer. Law Review*, Vol. XLIV

SOWERS, D. C. *Financial History of New York State, 1789–1912*, New York, 1914

STANWOOD, E. *American Tariff Controversies*, Boston, 1903

STRONG, M. M. *History of the Territory of Wisconsin*, Madison, 1885

SUMNER, W. G. *A History of American Currency*, New York, 1876

SUMNER, W. G. "A History of Banking in the United States," in a *History of Banking of All the Leading Nations*, New York, 1896

TAUSSIG, F. W. *Tariff History of the United States*, New York, 1905

THOMPSON, C. M. *The Illinois Whig before 1841*, in "University of Illinois Studies," Vol. IV

TRIMBLE, W. "Diverging Tendencies in New York Democracy in the Period of the Locofocos," in *Amer. Hist. Review*, April, 1919

TROTTER, A. *Observations on the Financial Position . . . . of the North American Union . . . . ,* London, 1839

UTLEY, H. N. "Wildcat Banking in Michigan," *Mich. Pioneer Collections*, Vol. V

WARD, G. W. *The Early Development of the Chesapeake and Ohio Project*, in "Johns Hopkins Studies," Vol. XVII

WAY, R. B. "Mississippi Valley and Internal Improvements, 1825–40," in *Mississippi Valley Historical Association Proceedings*, Vol. IV

WEAVER, C. C. *Internal Improvements in North Carolina previous to 1860*, in "Johns Hopkins Studies," Vol. XXI

WHITFORD, N. E. *History of the Canal System of the State of New York*, New York, 1906

WILDMAN, M. S. *Money Inflation in the United States*, Chicago, 1905

WOOLEN, E. "Labor Troubles, 1834–37," *Yale Review*, Vol. I

WORTHINGTON, T. K. "Historical Sketch of the Finances of Pennsylvania," in *Amer. Econ. Assoc. Pub.*, Vol. II

COLLECTIONS OF DOCUMENTS AND MAGAZINES

Blackwood's Magazine, Vol. XLII

Democratic Review, 1839–40

Green, E. B. and Thompson, C. N. (editors), *Governors' Letter Books*, in "Illinois Society Collections," Vol. II

Hunt's Merchants' Magazine, 1839–44

Lincoln, C. Z. *Messages of the Governors of New York*, Albany, 1909

New York Annual Register, 1837

North American Review, Vol. LI

RICHARDSON, J. D., *Messages and Papers of the Presidents*, Washington, 1896

Whig Almanac, 1836–38

GENERAL WORKS

BOLLES, A. *A Financial History of the United States*, New York, 1894

COMAN, K. *The Industrial History of the United States*, New York, 1910

DEWEY, D. R. *Financial History of the United States*, New York, 1909

HART, A. B. *Slavery and Abolition*, New York, 1906

MACDONALD, W. *Jacksonian Democracy*, New York, 1906

MCMASTER, J. D. *History of the People of the United States*, New York, 1888–1913

INDEX

Adams, J. Q., 179, 192, 200, 203

Agriculture, affected by internal improvements, 35, 36; increased interest, 104, 105; diversified crops, 114, 115, 117, 122, 124, 126, 127; prices, 175; affected by panic, 113, 114, 115, 116, 117, 118, 119, 123, 124, 125, 126, 127

Alabama, 49; internal improvements, 20, 21; banking operations, 26; affected by panic, 116; politics, 160, 163, 168

Albany, banks suspension, 93

Antimasons, 71, 76, 77, 78, 88, 90

Arkansas, 49; banking operations, 38, 39; affected by panic, 128; politics, 163

Augusta, banks suspension, 93

Baker, C. S., 228

Baltimore, banks suspension, 93

Baltimore and Ohio, 112, 113

Bank convention, 185, 186, 187, 198, 199, 201

Bank of England, 41, 199, 204, 206

Banking laws, 121, 122

Banks, 14; attitude toward, 135–38; growth of, 13, 16, 24, 25, 26, 27; defense of, 95, 96; deposits, 44; operations, 14–16, 24–27, 36–39, 92, 93; suspension, 93, 97, 99, 119; failures, 5, 119; banking

practices, 14, 15, 16, 17, 24–27, 36–39; expansion of credit, 6, 14, 16, 17, 19, 22, 26, 37, 107; *see also* United States Bank and United States Bank of Pennsylvania

Beardstown, 30

Benton, T. H., 210

Biddle, N., characterization, 1; versus Jackson, 2, 4–6, 13, 49; on Specie Circular, 67–69; recharter of United States Bank by Pennsylvania, 70–81, 85–88, 90; justifies bank, 94–96; on New York conditions, 96; retirement, 102, 204; on politics and political activities, 144, 148, 158, 162, 163, 172, 173, 201, 219, 225, 226, 228–31, 236; on resumption, 177–81, 184, 187–90, 192, 194, 200, 201, 202

Blair, F. P., 218, 223, 234

Boom cities, 54, 55, 56

Boston, 14

Bribery bill, 70

Brisbane, A., 136

Brockenbrough, Dr., 209, 210

Bryant, W. C., 150

Buchanan, J., 64, 146, 174, 225, 227, 228

Business, in East, 7–18; South, 18–28; West, 28–40; failures of business houses, 4, 96, 97, 98, 118; hardships, 96–113, 116–18, 126–27, 131, 133, 141, 142, 206, 207, 232; busi-

255

ness expansion, 7, 8, 9, 28, 29, 204, 205

Calhoun, J. C., 20, 89, 147, 158, 172, 176, 213, 216, 217, 223–25, 227–30

Canals, 9, 10, 12, 13, 17, 19, 21, 22, 30–34, 103, 112–14, 128–30; see also Internal improvements

Charleston, 93

Chesapeake and Ohio, 21, 22, 112, 113

Chicago, 29, 54

Cincinnati, 28, 29, 93, 124, 125

Clay, H., 216, 217, 219, 224–29, 233

Cloud, N. B., 115

Colt, R. L., 45

Connecticut, 8, 15; panic, 108; politics, 163, 167, 171

Conrad, H. W., 82–85

Cooper, T., 148

Cotton, 8, 18, 19, 102, 108, 119, 159, 205

Covington, 29

Crops, 3, 92, 103, 116, 123, 123 n., 124, 126, 127; see also Agriculture and Cotton

Dayton, 29

Debtors, 101, 106, 119, 120, 121, 125, 127, 139

Delaware, 72, 186

Democrats, 77–79, 82, 90, 145–58, 161, 163–66, 172, 175, 214, 216, 225, 228, 232

Deposit banks, 92

Deposits, removal of, 3

Detroit, 29

District of Columbia, 93

Dunn, J. L., 82

Elections, 1832, 3; 1837, 152–63, table, 163; 1838, 163–72; 1839, 172, 173; preparations for 1840, 173–75

England, relations with United States, 40–42

Erie Canal, 9, 10

Evans, G. H., 150

Ewing, T., 89

Exports, 19, 40, 92, 142, 160, 161; see also Imports

Florida, 26, 27; panic, 120, 121

Fort Sheldon, 55

Gallatin, A., 198

Georgia, 20, 27, 49; panic, 120, 121; politics, 158, 163, 168, 169

Girard, S., 222

Girard Bank, 16, 17

Grundy, F., 199, 225, 227

Hamer's resolution, 197–99

Hammond, J. H., 115, 159

Harrison, W. H., 219

Hartford, 93

Hayne, R. Y., 19

Hessian fly, 92

Hone, P., 45

Humphreys and Biddle, 182, 204, 205

Hunter, R. M. T., 232

Illinois, 28, 123; internal improvements, 30–32, 125, 128, 129; banking operations, 38; land sales, 53–56; panic, 123, 125, 126, 128, 129; politics, 170, 171

Immigration, 18

Imports, 40, 92, 142; see also Exports

Independent Treasury, 2, 147–49, 158, 162, 172, 175, 191, 201, 209–36

Indiana, 28; internal improvements, 33, 34; banking operations, 39; panic, 126; politics, 161, 163, 171, 172

Internal improvements, 9, 10–13, 16, 17, 19, 21, 22, 24, 30–35, 70, 103, 112–14, 128–30; *see also* Canals

Ireland, 41

Jackson, A., 6, 44, 64, 213, 216, 234–36; political philosophy, 1; contest with Biddle, 2; messages, 2; charter of United States Bank of Pennsylvania, 89; politics, 158, 160, 176

Jaudon, S., 23, 182, 200

Jerome, C., 111

Jones, J. V., 115

Journal of American Railways, 7

Juneau, S., 133

Kankakee, 54

Kendall, A., 225

Kentucky, 49; internal improvements, 23; banking operations, 26; panic, 123, 126, 128, 130; politics, 161, 163

Krebs, Col. J., 82–85

Labor, 4, 9, 19, 98, 130–34; internal improvements, 35, 36; relations with banks, 95, 96; wages in 1840, 174; *see also* Panic

Land, 91, 92; *see* Speculation

Land offices, 50–52, 59, 60; *see also* Speculation

Leggett, W., 150

Locofoco, 136, 149–51, 157, 163, 164, 166, 172, 176, 211, 213, 221

Louisiana, 21, 48, 49; panic, 118–20; politics, 170, 171

Louisville, 29, 93

Lytle, R. T., 57

McIlvaine, J., 73, 74, 77, 80, 81, 85–88

Maine, 14, 47; politics, 163, 167, 172

Marcy, W. L., 198; messages, 17, 46, 47, 100, 103; on politics, 154, 155, 165

Martineau, H., 45

Maryland, 72, 79, 80; internal improvements, 22, 23; panic, 112, 113; politics, 160, 163, 168, 171, 172

Massachusetts, manufactures, 8; internal improvements, 12; banks, 13; banking capital, 13, 14; banking operations, 15; panic, 131; politics, 156, 163, 166, 167, 171, 172

Michigan, 28; internal improvements, 34, 35; banking operations, 36, 38; politics, 163

Mississippi, 48; internal improvements, 21; banking operations and laws, 25, 26, 122; land sales, 49–52; panic, 116–18; politics, 158, 163, 168, 171

Missouri, 28, 30

Mobile, 93

Moore, E., 135, 222

Nashville, 29

New Haven, 93

New Jersey, 72, 108; politics, 163, 171, 172

New Orleans, 93, 118–20

New York, real estate, 3, 6, 45–47; manufacturers, 7, 9; internal improvements, 9–11, 103, 104; governor's messages, 10, 11, 12, 17, 46, 47, 198; banks, 14, 71, 72, 79, 93, 99, 100, 101–3, 183, 188, 190, 191, 196; politics, 150, 151, 153–56, 163–66, 171, 172; *see also* Panic and Speculation

New York City, 11; business in, 17, 18; fire, 93; banks suspension, 97, stop and tax law, 104; politics, 149, 150; *see* Panic and Speculation

Newport, 29

North Carolina, internal improvements, 20; panic, 112, 113; politics, 160, 163, 168, 171, 172

Nullification, 2

Ohio, 28; internal improvements, 32, 33, 130; banking operations, 38; panic, 123, 124, 125, 127; politics, 161, 163, 171

Owen, R., 136

Panic of 1833–34, 3, 4

Panic of 1837, 1–7, 90, 103; extent, 1, 2; *Bank of United States* v. *Government*, 2; *Jackson* v. *Biddle*, 2, 3; business failures, 4, 96, 98, 118; labor, 4, 9, 19, 35, 36, 98, 130–34; wages, 4, 9; bank failures, 5, 119; distribution of surplus revenue, 6; expansion of credit, 6, 14, 16, 19, 22, 24, 26, 27, 36; Specie Circular, 6, 61–68; business expansion, 7–9, 28, 29; internal improvements, 9–13, 16, 17, 19–24, 30–35, 103, 112–14, 128, 129, 130; worthless currency, 16, 17, 37; speculation, 17, 43–48, 50, 52–60; irregular banking transactions, 14–17, 24–27, 36–39; imports and exports, 19, 40, 92, 142; foreign indebtedness, 40, 41; public lands, 44, 48, 49, 50–52, 56, 59, 60, 65, 66; disappearance of specie, 63, 99; fundamental causes, 91–93; banks suspensions, 93–119; contemporary opinion, 93–94; effect on states: Alabama, 116, Arkansas, 128, Connecticut, 108, Delaware, 108, Florida, 120, 121, Georgia, 120, 121, Illinois, 123, 125, 127–30, Indiana, 123, 125, 126, 130, Kentucky, 126, 128, 130, Louisiana, 118, 119, 120, Maryland, 112, 113, Michigan, 127, 130, Mississippi, 115, 116, 118, New Hampshire, 105, 106, 107, New Jersey, 108, New York, 96–105, North Carolina, 112, 113, 118, Ohio, 123, 124, 127, 130, Pennsylvania, 108, 110, South Carolina, 112–15, Tennessee, 128, 130, Vermont, 107, 108, Virginia, 112, 113, Wisconsin, 127; havoc wrought, 96–112, 140–43; prices, 98, 99; effect, 104, 110–12, 123, 128, 129, 130, 132, 133, 142–44; prices on negroes, 116–18; loss of confidence, 138–40; and politics, 145–76

Panic of 1839, 102, 110, 114, 119, 123, 126, 127, 204, 205, 206, 207, 232

Patterson, B., 82, 83

Pennsylvania, manufactures, 7; canals, 12; internal improve-

ments, 12, 13, 70; banks, 16;
panic, 108–11; politics, 71,
74, 75, 163, 171, 172; *see also*
Biddle, United States Bank
of Pennsylvania and Re-
sumption

Penrose, C. B., 80

Philadelphia, 7, 13, 94, 183,
184–87, 189, 190, 196, 201

Philips, M. W., 115

Pickens, F. W., 220–22

Pittsburgh, 13, 29

Poinsett, J. R., 67, 178

Polk, J. K., 173, 212, 225

Pontotoc, 49

Providence, 93

Public lands, 5, 6, 43–70, 91,
92; *see also* Speculation

Quincy, 12

Railroads, 12, 17, 22; *see also*
Internal improvements

Real estate, 3, 6, 17, 18; *see*
Speculation

Reed, W. R., 72, 74

Registers, instructions to, 58, 59

Repudiation, 118, 121

Resumption, 100, 108, 114,
177; *see also* United States
Bank and Resumption

Rhode Island, 157; politics,
163, 171, 172

Ritchie, T., 146, 169, 170

Ritner, J., 70, 71, 73, 77, 87, 88,
167, 201, 222

Rives, W. C., 148, 158, 210,
213–18, 224, 225

Ruffin, E., 115

St. Louis, 29, 30

Sergeant, J., 196, 229

Seward, W. H., 11, 101, 103,
104

South Carolina, internal improvements, 17, 18; panic,
112–15; politics, 168, 171,
172

Specie Circular, 42, 61–69, 192,
229; issued, 6, 61, 92; motives
for, 61, 62; results, 62–64, 94,
160; drafting, 89; repealed,
200

Specie payments, 41, 100, 108,
114, 120, 177, 198; *see* Banks

Speculation, 17, 18, 40, 43–70,
94, 102; *see also* Lands, Real
estate, and Panic

Stevens, T., 71, 73, 76, 77, 79,
87, 88

Strong, M. M., 57, 133

Sub-treasury; *see* Independent
Treasury

Surplus revenue, distribution
of, 6, 92, 93, 94

Tallmadge, N. P., 148, 210,
213, 216, 218, 219

Taney, R., 160, 161

Tennessee, internal improvements, 23, 24; banks, 26;
panic, 128; politics, 161,
163, 172

United States, conditions in,
1830, 2; 1833, 3; 1835, 5;
eastern section: conditions,
7–18; real estate and land
sales, 45–48; industrial and
financial aspects, 96–112,
130–33; southern sections:
conditions in, 18–28; real
estate, 48–52; financial and
industrial aspects, 112–23;
western section: 28–40; land
sales, 52–56; financial and

industrial aspects, 123–30; *see also* Panic

United States Bank (Second), 1, 3–5, 70, 91, 93

United States Bank of Pennsylvania, 69; chartered, 70–91; drafting bill, 71–74; introduction of bill, 74; popular attitude toward, 75–79; provisions of bill, 75–77; bill in House, 74–78; investigation, 81–85; bill in Senate, 80–87; enacted, 88; federal and state reactions, 89; suspension of, 94, 95, 207; cotton speculations, 102, 181, 182, 183, 205, 206; resumption, 181; attitude on resumption, 177–81

Van Buren, M., 1, 2, 64, 87, 175, 180, 196, 203, 207, 210, 219, 224, 228, 231, 232; on Specie Circular, 63, 65–67, 69; on Locofocos, 136, 141; on Independent Treasury, 144, 162, 169; on politics, 145, 173; appeal to people, 148; messages, 152, 157; refuses aid, 178, 179

Vermont, banking operations, 15; panic, 107, 108; politics, 163, 171, 172

Vicksburg, 48

Virginia, internal improvements, 21, 22; panic, 113, 114; politics, 158, 171

Wallace, J. B., 85

Webster, D., 90, 216, 217, 218, 219, 226, 227

Whig, 71, 76, 77, 78, 82, 87, 88, 90, 144, 147, 151, 154, 155–60, 163–66, 170–72, 176, 214, 219, 225, 232

Women, wages, 8, 9

Woodbury, L., 198, 199, 200, 203

Wright, S., 210, 213, 224, 233

Zanesville, 59

PHOENIX BOOKS

in Political Science and Law

P 4   *F. A. Hayek:* The Road to Serfdom

P 5   *Jacques Maritain:* Man and the State

P 27   *Daniel J. Boorstin:* The Genius of American Politics

P 67   *Yves R. Simon:* Philosophy of Democratic Government

P 84   *Edward H. Levi:* An Introduction to Legal Reasoning

P 97   *Gertrude Himmelfarb:* Lord Acton: A Study in Conscience and Politics

P 111 *Milton Friedman:* Capitalism and Freedom

P 112 *Leo Strauss:* The Political Philosophy of Hobbes: Its Basis and Its Genesis

P 113 *Carl Brent Swisher:* The Growth of Constitutional Power in the United States

P 115 *Robert A. Dahl:* A Preface to Democratic Theory

P 116 *Sebastian de Grazia:* The Political Community: A Study of Anomie

P 120 *F. A. Hayek,* EDITOR: Capitalism and the Historians

P 121 *Bertrand de Jouvenel:* Sovereignty: An Inquiry into the Political Good

P 130 *Walter J. Blum and Harry Kalven, Jr.:* The Uneasy Case for Progressive Taxation

P 135 *Carl Joachim Friedrich:* The Philosophy of Law in Historical Perspective

P 137 *Dallin H. Oaks,* EDITOR: The Wall between Church and State

P 143 *Karl Jaspers:* The Future of Mankind

P 144 *Forrest McDonald:* We the People

P 152 *Allison Dunham and Philip B. Kurland,* EDITORS: Mr. Justice

P 160 *Robert Endicott Osgood:* Ideals and Self-Interest in America's Foreign Relations

P 168 *Henry Bamford Parkes:* Marxism: An Autopsy

P 174 *Morris Janowitz:* The Military in the Political Development of New Nations

PHOENIX BOOKS
in History

P 2   *Edward Chiera:* They Wrote on Clay

P 11   *John A. Wilson:* The Culture of Ancient Egypt

P 13   *Ernest Staples Osgood:* The Day of the Cattleman

P 16   *Karl Löwith:* Meaning in History: The Theological Implications of the Philosophy of History

P 22   *Euclides da Cunha:* Rebellion in the Backlands

P 27   *Daniel J. Boorstin:* The Genius of American Politics

P 28   *David M. Potter:* People of Plenty: Economic Abundance and the American Character

P 29   *Eleanor Shipley Duckett:* Alfred the Great: The King and His England

P 36   *A. T. Olmstead:* History of the Persian Empire

P 40   *Giorgio de Santillana:* The Crime of Galileo

P 61   *Warren S. Tryon:* My Native Land: Life in America, 1790–1870

P 66   *Alan Simpson:* Puritanism in Old and New England

P 69   *Gustave E. von Grunebaum:* Medieval Islam

P 70   *Oscar Jászi:* Dissolution of the Habsburg Monarchy

P 73   *Howard H. Peckham:* Pontiac and the Indian Uprising

P 80   *Carl Bridenbaugh:* The Colonial Craftsman

P 125 *George Steindorff and Keith C. Seele:* When Egypt Ruled the East

P 144 *Forrest McDonald:* We the People: The Economic Origins of the Constitution

P 147 *Donald Culross Peattie:* Venice: Immortal Village

P 150 *Kenneth Stampp:* And the War Came: The North and the Secession Crisis, 1860–61

P 153 *Eric L. McKitrick:* Andrew Johnson and Reconstruction

P 156–157   *Marc Bloch:* Feudal Society, *Vols I and II*

P 161 *Richard C. Wade:* The Urban Frontier: Pioneer Life in Early Pittsburgh, Cincinnati, Lexington, Louisville, and St. Louis

P 163 *Ernest K. Bramsted:* Aristocracy and the Middle-Classes in Germany

P 165 *Almont Lindsey:* The Pullman Strike

P 166 *William H. McNeill:* Past and Future

P 167 *Muhsin Mahdi:* Ibn Khaldûn's Philosophy of History

P 168 *Henry Bamford Parkes:* Marxism: An Autopsy